MUSIC THEORY
RESOURCE BOOK

Harold Owen
School of Music
The University of Oregon

New York   Oxford
OXFORD UNIVERSITY PRESS
2000

Oxford University Press

Oxford   New York
Athens   Auckland   Bangkok   Bogotá   Buenos Aires   Calcutta
Cape Town   Chennai   Dar es Salaam   Delhi   Florence   Hong Kong   Istanbul
Karachi   Kuala Lumpur   Madrid   Melbourne   Mexico City   Mumbai
Nairobi   Paris   São Paulo   Singapore   Taipei   Tokyo   Toronto   Warsaw

and associated companies in
Berlin   Ibadan

Published by Oxford University Press, Inc.
198 Madison Avenue, New York, New York 10016
http://www.oup-usa.org

Oxford is a registered trademark of Oxford University Press

Library of Congress Cataloging-in-Publication Data

Owen, Harold.
  Music theory resource book / Harold Owen.
     p.   cm.

  ISBN 978-0-19-511539-0

  1. Music—Theory.   I. Title.
MT6.088M87   2000
781—dc21   99-21158
                                                          CIP

Printing (last digit): 9 8

Printed in the United States of America
on acid-free paper

Contents

Preface

This book is offered as a resource of musical examples, information, and exercises for first- and second-year college music theory courses and for graduate courses in theory review. The musical examples at the beginning of each chapter are for the most part complete compositions. They can serve as a basic anthology and as the focus for the discussion questions that follow them. The information is given succinctly in outline form, which can serve as a point of departure for the instructor's own style of explanation and demonstration. The outline format will be useful to the students for reference and review. The exercises at the end of each chapter offer a variety of tasks ranging in difficulty from easier ones, designed for all students, to others marked with an asterisk, intended for students with more extensive background, higher skills, and talent. Some are analytical, while others offer problems in scoring, arranging, or simple composition.

Several features not normally found in basic theory texts are a summary of basic acoustics, standard notation practices, music in two and three parts (including the basic principles of counterpoint), jazz harmony, techniques borrowed from musics of non-Western cultures, and two chapters on techniques developed in the twentieth century (Chapter 19 deals with music from 1900–1950; Chapter 20 deals with music since 1950). The musical examples represent a wide variety of periods and genres, including, for example, a mass movement by Josquin des Prez, a Russian folk tune, the lead sheet of a popular song, a humorous choral piece by William Billings, a North Indian raga, variations by Beethoven and Brahms, a chromatic motet by Lassus, and an organ work from the 1980s by Messiaen. Bach, Schumann, Chopin, Mozart, Franck, Debussy, Bartók, Hindemith, Dallapiccola, Stravinsky, Crumb, and Pärt also are represented, as well as several examples I composed especially for this book.

While *Music Theory Resource Book* is not intended as a primary resource in the area of music history, it discusses styles of various periods and examines types of music from all major periods, jazz and folk music, and musics of non-Western cultures. The Style Profiles in Appendix A can provide students with a historical perspective of styles in terms of the musical dimensions of pulse, rhythm and meter, melody, harmony, tonality, genres and structures, texture, and color. For those interested in figured bass realization, Appendix B gives details on this subject using as an example a continuo realization of the opening of the Trio Sonata from *The Musical Offering*, done by a student of Bach.

Analysis is generally limited to the basic building blocks of "musical grammar," but also extends to structural units (motive, subphrase, phrase, period, and small forms). A summary of the basic configuration of larger forms is included. Analytical techniques such as those developed by Schenker, LaRue, and Forte are not discussed, since students will meet them in courses on form and analysis.

Suggestions for the Student

Before a chapter is to be taken up by the class, study each of the examples carefully. Play them on the piano or sing the various parts if you can. See how many of the discussion questions you can answer. Then study the *Definitions, Principles, and Observations* given, and jot down items you wish to have explained more fully in class. Take an active part in the class discussions, and don't be afraid to ask questions. Take part in the class performances of the examples and exercises. Before you hand in your assigned work, make sure you have checked it carefully for clear and proper notation (or good English when asked for prose responses).

Suggestions for the Instructor

Whenever possible, have the class perform, or play recordings of the examples at the beginning of each chapter. Be prepared with additional examples. Use the discussion questions to focus the students on the principles exemplified in the music. The information in the *Definitions, Principles, and Observations* sections have been kept concise, inviting you to explain, amplify, and demonstrate in your own way. Make careful and appropriate assignment of exercises. You may wish to choose from those given. Those marked with an asterisk are for those students ready for special challenges. You may wish to invite students to do them for extra credit. I have found that students appreciate a touch of humor from time to time, and you will find it in several of the exercises.

If you are using this book as a secondary text, you will find the musical examples, discussion questions, and exercises useful. The text information can be used for review and summary. Since the chapters are relatively self-contained, you can select materials in whatever order works best with your primary text and your own preferences.

If you are using this book for a graduate theory review course, a comprehensive diagnostic test given at the beginning of the course will indicate the students' strengths and weaknesses. Some chapters can be covered quickly, and some will need in-depth study. Assignments can be a sampling of the easier and the more challenging exercises. Your students are likely to have very diverse skills and knowledge; you may wish to assign different exercises to different students. A lively discussion among the students, each contributing his or her own knowledge and experience, can be much more valuable than pure lecture.

Part One

CHAPTER 1

THE NATURE OF MUSIC

Study these scores as you consider the questions that follow them.

Example 1-1 Von fremden Ländern und Menschen from *Kinderszenen*, Op. 15 by Robert Schumann (1810–1856).

Example 1-2 Jazz solo on "Cherokee" by Charlie Parker (1920–1955), transcribed by Carl Woideck. (Used by permission of Carl Woideck.)

Example 1-3 *"to the last drop"* from *visible musics* by William Hellerman (b. 1939) (© 1973 by William Hellermann—All rights reserved. Parts available through American Composers Alliance, 170 W. 74th St., NY, NY 10023. *"to the last drop"* for six mallet instruments by William Hellermann. This piece is one of a series of works with the group title, *Eye Scores*. First performed at the Kitchen performance space in New York City, 1978, by six vibraphones positioned around the perimeter of the space. A realization of the score can include taped sounds of water and visuals relating to water.)

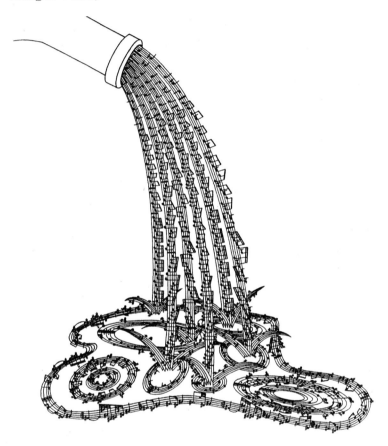

QUESTIONS FOR DISCUSSION

1. What is music? How would you describe it to an English-speaking alien?

2. Name as many kinds of music as you can. What kinds are written down and what kinds are not?

3. What kinds of music are made up on the spot?

4. What is an arrangement?

5. What is music made of—what are its elements or dimensions?

6. What is meant by *musical style?*

7. What is meant by *musical texture?*

8. How do we know what music was like before our own century?

9. Most music we know requires three types of musicians: a composer, one or more performers, and an audience. Can you think of music that alters this formula?

10. How do each of the examples above fit your definition of music? of style? of texture?

DEFINITIONS, PRINCIPLES, AND OBSERVATIONS

A. DEFINITIONS. Music has been defined in many ways. Some are physical, some are esthetic, some are philosophical, others are practical. Here are several definitions to consider and discuss:

   1. An art of sound in time which expresses ideas and emotions in significant forms through the elements of rhythm, melody, harmony, and color.[1]

   2. Sounds and silences organized by pitch, duration, loudness, and timbre

   3. The notated score

   4. Sounds one wishes to hear (music) as opposed to sounds one does not wish to hear (noise)

   5. Universal order (as in "the music of the spheres")

   6. An element of religious or ceremonial rites in cultures throughout the world

   7. A commodity to aid in selling products, promoting political messages, soothing passengers and patients, filling silence, and banishing boredom

B. DIMENSIONS. Traditional music theory considers the elements of music to be *melody, harmony, rhythm, tone color,* and *form*. A more comprehensive approach gives the following four musical dimensions:

   1. *Temporal dimension*: pulse, beat, meter, rhythm, rhythmic density, tempo

   2. *Pitch dimension*: melody, harmony, tonality, tessitura, temperament

   3. *Structural dimension*: motive, subphrase, phrase, phrase group, period, section, exposition, repetition, variation, development, and other formal units, textural continuity

   4. *Color dimension*: timbre, dynamics, articulation

   Terms associated with each of these dimensions will be explored in detail in subsequent chapters.

C. STYLE. Style refers to characteristics that define period, genre, region, an individual or group of composers, or manner of performance. The Style Profiles you will find in Appendix A describe various style periods in terms of the four musical dimensions.

D. TEXTURE. Musical texture results from the interaction of the temporal and pitch dimensions. Terms most often used to define texture are homophony, polyphony, heterophony, and simultaneity. Other words often used to describe texture are thin, thick, simple, complex, varied, homogeneous, layered, contrapuntal, and patterned. Texture is discussed in depth in Chapter 11.

---

[1]*The Random House Dictionary of the English Language*. Ed.: Jess Stein. Random House, N. Y. 1967.

E. SOURCES. Not all music comes to us from the pen of a dead composer. Some of it is improvised on the spot, and sometimes we are asked to create it given a few directions. The following will be useful in the classification of musical sources:

1. *Composed music.* Music created by a known or anonymous composer, usually available in standard notation.

2. *Arrangements and settings.* Works based on preexisting music.

3. *Folk music.* Music belonging to cultural traditions and ceremonies, usually created by unknown composers. Folk music is subject to interpretation by performers and may or may not be available in notation.

4. *Improvisation.* Music created by one or more performers in real time.

5. *Indeterminacy.* Music that is determined wholly or in part by the choices made by performers or their interpretation of nonstandard notation.

6. *Aleatory music.* Music in which choices are made by chance, such as the rolling of dice or a random number generator.

EXERCISES

EXERCISE 1-1 Write a short essay in which you discuss each of the seven definitions of music given in the outline. Discuss their application and appropriateness. Give your own personal definition of music.

EXERCISE 1-2 List one or two musical examples (genres or specific compositions) that fit each of the descriptions below.

a. The pitch dimension is of primary importance; temporal dimension is of little consequence.

b. The temporal dimension is of primary importance; pitch dimension is of little consequence.

c. The color dimension is of primary importance.

d. There is no discernible regular feeling of "beat" or "pulse."

e. The structural dimension consists of endless repetitions of musical patterns.

f. There is melody, but no harmony.

g. The harmony is far more important than the melody.

EXERCISE 1-3 Describe in a few words the role played by each of the four dimensions in the three examples at the beginning of this chapter. Classify each of them according to its musical source. Do the same for as many of the following genres as you can.

a. hymn (such as "Onward Christian soldiers")

b. toccata for keyboard instrument

c. Viennese waltz

d. fugue for brass

e. jazz played by a small combo

f. Native American dance

g. piano rag music

h. "elevator music"

i. rap music

j. gamelan music

NOTE: The asterisks below and for subsequent exercises in each chapter indicate exercises intended for students with a more advanced background of skills and knowledge and for those using the book for review purposes.

*EXERCISE 1-4 Choose two of the composers listed below and write a paragraph or two describing their style in terms of the four dimensions of music.

    a. Steve Reich

    b. Frank Zappa

    c. Anton Webern

    d. Hildegarde von Bingen

    e. Olivier Messiaen

    f. Claude Debussy

*EXERCISE 1-5 Explain how the score below can be used as the basis for a composition. Begin at the left and proceed clockwise.

CHAPTER 2

THE PHYSICAL PROPERTIES OF MUSIC

QUESTIONS FOR DISCUSSION

1. What is sound? How is it transmitted? How do we perceive it?

2. How are tones physically different from noise?

3. How would you describe sound waves? What is the difference between waves that communicate to us louder compared to softer sounds? What is the difference between waves that communicate higher compared to lower pitches? Can you describe waves that are produced by a noise source such as freeway traffic?

4. A above Middle C is tuned to 440 Hz. (Hertz). What does that mean?

5. When two clarinettists are trying to play the same pitch, but they sound "out of tune," how do we sense this? During an orchestra's tuning-up, how does the concertmaster know when his or her A string is in tune with the oboe? Once the A is in tune, how does a violinist tune the other strings?

6. What is it that makes an alto saxophone sound different from a clarinet? How can we tell whether we are hearing a tone from a piano, a harp, or a guitar?

7. Why does choral music sound different when sung in a church compared to an open field? Can you explain why blowing on an empty bottle produces a lower tone than blowing on the same bottle half filled with water?

8. When a singer uses vibrato, what is changing—pitch, loudness, tone quality?

9. Why is it essential that musicians have a basic understanding of acoustics?

DEFINITIONS, PRINCIPLES, AND OBSERVATIONS

The following outline gives a brief explanation of the most basic concepts and terms encountered in the physics of sound and music.

A. SOUND GENERATION AND PROPAGATION

1. Sound is generated by vibrating objects such as strings, reeds, membranes, columns of air, wood, and metal.

2. The vibrations create waves that travel through the air (or some other adjacent medium). Sound waves radiate outwards through the air in expanding spheres—unless they are absorbed or reflected. Their energy is diminished as they expand.

3. The ear intercepts the sound waves, then converts them into nerve impulses that the brain interprets.

B. PROPERTIES OF WAVES

1. A wave has a crest and a trough. As it travels through air, molecules are first pushed together, making the crest or *condensation*; then they are stretched apart, making the trough or *rarefaction*. The part of a wave from one crest to the next is called a *cycle*. Frequency is usually given in cycles per second or Hertz (Hz.). A above middle C on a piano is usually tuned to a frequency of 440 Hz.

2. Waves that move faster are closer together; waves that move slower are farther apart. *Frequency* is the number of waves that pass a point in one second. We interpret frequency as *pitch*.

3. The distance between crests is called the *wave length*. The higher the frequency, the shorter the wave length; the lower the frequency, the longer the wave length.

4. When there is a big difference in the density of molecules at the crest compared to the trough, the wave (and the sound) have high energy. This difference is the *amplitude* of the wave. We interpret amplitude as loudness (volume, or intensity).

Example 2-1 The anatomy of a sine wave.

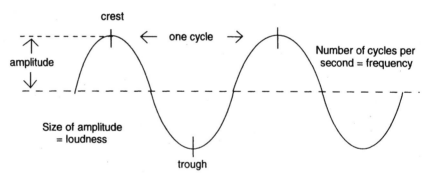

5. When waves come regularly in time, they are called *periodic* (or *harmonic*) and produce tones. If they come randomly in time, they are called *aperiodic* and produce noise.

C. AMPLIFICATION, RESONANCE, AND REVERBERATION

1. If a vibrating string is attached to a solid object, such as a violin body or a sound board, the vibration is intensified or amplified. A tuning fork sounds much louder if you hold it against a wooden surface.

2. If the sound waves fit comfortably in an enclosed space, they are intensified. This is called *resonance*. The tubes beneath the bars on a marimba or vibraphone are called resonators. Each one is cut precisely to half the wave length produced by its associated bar.

3. When the enclosed space is short, the resonant wave will have a short wave length and a high frequency. As the length of the space is extended, a lower frequency will be produced. When a flutist plays middle C, all holes are covered. The C an octave higher is produced when the first open hole is half way along the flute.

4. A well-designed concert hall provides resonance and reflection of sound waves at all frequencies. Resonance and reflection can combine to produces *reverberation*.

5. Sound is reflected best by hard surfaces such as stone or glass. It is absorbed by porous or soft surfaces such as cork or cloth. In a large enclosed space with hard surfaces, the sound energy takes longer to dissipate than it does in a comparable space with soft surfaces. A choir singing in a cathedral sounds "live" to us, but would sound "dead" to us in a hotel lobby.

D. TONE QUALITY OR TIMBRE

1. The shape of a wave affects its tone quality or timbre. The *sine wave* is the simplest wave form. The tone it produces is a very pure "oo" sound, as in the word "too." The "a" sound, as in the word "tape," is produced by a very complex wave form.

2. Complex waves can be produced by the combination of many sine waves, all of which have frequencies which are whole-number multiples of a single frequency, called the *fundamental*.

3. The harmonic series is a set of pitches beginning with the fundamental frequency, f, plus its whole-number multiples, 2f, 3f, 4f, 5f, 6f, etc., continuing past audibility. These frequencies are called *partials* or *harmonics*. All frequencies except the fundamental are called *overtones* or *upper partials*.

Example 2-2 The harmonic or overtone series.

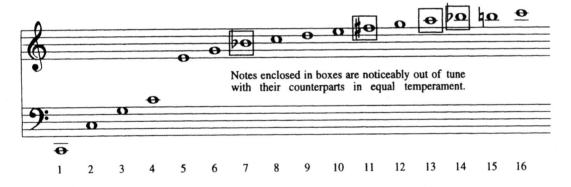

Notes enclosed in boxes are noticeably out of tune with their counterparts in equal temperament.

1   2   3   4   5   6   7   8   9   10   11   12   13   14   15   16

4. The selection and relative strength of overtones present in a tone gives it its characteristic tone color or timbre. The clarinet, for example, has strong odd-numbered partials. The flute has strong even-numbered partials.

5. Some instruments produce sounds that do not adhere closely to the harmonic series. These are the percussion instruments, such as drums, cymbals, and gongs. Membranophones tend to produce random frequencies within a small range. Metallophones produce tones that are not harmonically related.

E. ENVELOPE

1. A change in amplitude, frequency, or timbre during a tone is called the *envelope*. The envelope of a bell is an immediate attack, followed by a gradual decay, or *damping*, of the amplitude. A tone on a French horn may have a more gradual attack, sustain at one level for the duration of a note, then have

a quick release. A vibrato usually involves changes in both frequency and timbre. Portamento results in a gradual change in frequency.

2. Articulation in music involves adjustment of the envelope for a single note or a series of notes.

3. Dynamics affect the amplitude for a single note or a series of notes. A change in dynamic level often affects the timbre as well.

F. BEATS, INTERFERENCE, DIFFERENCE TONES

1. The interval of a third is generally considered to be a pleasing or consonant harmony. If the frequency of the upper tone is lowered gradually, we have the impression of an increasingly dissonant sonority until the two tones are quite close in frequency. When they are about ten cycles apart, we become aware of a pulsating sensation called *beats.*

2. When the two pitches are very close, the crests of their waves are aligned for an instant, producing a louder sound; then later the crest of one wave comes at the same time as the trough in the other, causing a nullifying of the sound. The beat rate is the difference in frequency. When tuning the strings for a particular key on the piano, the tuner listens for beats and adjusts the string until the beat rate is reduced to zero.

3. If two tones of the same frequency have their crests aligned constantly, they are *in phase.* If they are not aligned, they are *out of phase.* If they are exactly half a cycle out of phase, they can interfere with or nullify each other

4. When two high-pitched instruments are playing in close harmony at a high dynamic level, you become aware of some lower tones that are not actually being played by either of the instruments. These are *difference tones.* The frequency is equal to the difference between the frequencies of the tones being played.

G. INTERVALS AND CHORDS

1. Musicians use the term *interval* when expressing the difference in pitch between two tones. See Chapter 5 for a more complete discussion of intervals.

2. If you look at the harmonic series shown in Ex. 2-2, you can find most of the intervals as they are found in nature. The octave appears between the fundamental and the 2nd partial or harmonic. An octave can be expressed as a 2:1 ratio of frequencies. Similarly, the fifth appears to be between partials 2 and 3, a 3:2 frequency ratio. A 4:3 ratio produces a fourth; a 5:4 ratio produces a major third; a 6:5 ratio produces a minor third. Our major scale does not have a tone anywhere near the 7th partial, so we must move to a 9:8 ratio for a major second. A slightly smaller major second is produced by the ratio of 10:9. The closest approximation to our ears of a minor second would be a 16:15 ratio.

3. If we skip the 4th partial, we find a major sixth between partials 3 and 5, and a minor sixth between 5 and 8. Ratios of 15:8 and 16:9 are close to the major and minor sevenths, respectively.

4. A C major triad contains the tones C–E–G. Note that one appears in the harmonic series as partials 4–5–6. An E minor triad appears as partials 10–12–15.

H. TEMPERAMENT AND TUNING

1. If you tried to build a complete major scale using pitches from the overtones of any C, you would find a pretty good D (9th partial), E (5th partial), G (3rd partial), A (13th partial, but rather flat), and B (15th partial, also flat). To get anything close to F, you would have to go all the way to partial number 21. You would have to "temper" your tuning. If you tune tones to their overtone equivalents, you have *just tuning.*

2. Throughout history there have been many methods to achieve good tuning. Some of these gave very good results for some scales but disastrous results for others. By 1700, a method of tuning called *equal temperament* was introduced. It did not become the standard for tuning, however, until the middle of the nineteenth century.

3. Equal temperament is a compromise, in which each of the half steps of the chromatic scale has the same ratio of frequencies. In just tuning, a half step is produced by the ratio of 16:15; the upper frequency is 1.067 times larger than the lower frequency. In equal temperament, the upper frequency is 1.059 times the lower frequency. The fifths are slightly smaller, the fourths and major thirds are slightly larger than in just tuning.

4. *Cents.* Acousticians have found it convenient to measure intervals in cents. There are 100 cents in each semitone ("half step") in equal temperament. 200 cents = a major second. A minor third = 300 cents. Continuing in the same manner, the octave (twelve semitones) = 1200 cents.

FREQUENCIES OF NOTES IN THE CHROMATIC SCALE IN EQUAL TEMPERAMENT BEGINNING ON MIDDLE C (ROUNDED TO FOUR FIGURES)

Pitch name	C	C♯/D♭	D	D♯/E♭	E	F	F♯/G♭	G	G♯/A♭	A	A♯/B♭	B
Frequency	261.6	277.2	293.7	311.1	329.6	349.2	370.0	392.0	415.3	440.0	466.2	493.9

I. OCTAVE DESIGNATION

1. In the Middle Ages, the following names were given to notes beginning on bottom-line G in bass clef and continuing up to top-space E in treble clef:

   Γ A B c d e f g a b c′ d′ e′ f′ g′ a′ b′ c″ d″ e″.

2. In the mid-nineteenth century, the great German physicist Hermann Helmholtz proposed a system for octave designation, still widely used today, which extends the medieval scale in both directions (see the first row under the staff in Ex. 2-3.)

3. In 1940 the Acoustical Society of America adopted the system shown in the second row (USA Standard). C_1 is the lowest C on the piano.

4. Piano tuners number all keys on the piano counting from the lowest (A_1) to the highest (C_{88}).

5. Organ builders use still another system. In addition, organists refer to registers using pipe-length designations. If the largest pipe in a rank of pipes is about 8 ft. in length, it will produce CC (two octaves below Middle C). For 8 ft. stops, Middle C is the same pitch for the organ as for the piano. With 4 ft. stops, if you press Middle C, the resulting sound is an octave higher. With 2 ft. stops, it is two octaves higher. With 16 ft. stops, it is an octave lower; and with 32 ft. stops, it is two octaves lower.

6. Digital musical instruments and computers use MIDI (Musical Instrument Digital Interface) to communicate with each other. Pitches are represented by numbers. Middle C is MIDI note 60.

7. We also use informal designations. *Middle C* is located on the first ledger line below the treble staff and the first ledger line above the bass staff. *Low C* is two ledger lines below the bass staff, and *High C* is two ledger lines above the treble staff.

Example 2-3 Various systems for octave designation.

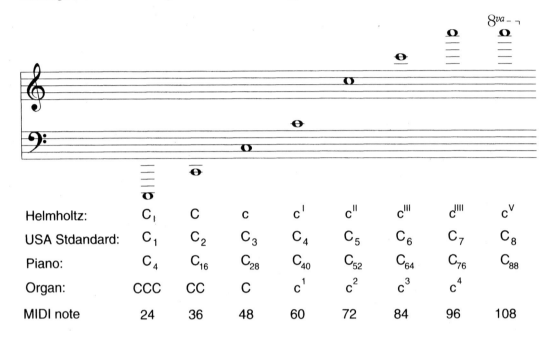

Helmholtz:	C_1	C	c	c^I	c^{II}	c^{III}	c^{IIII}	c^V
USA Stdandard:	C_1	C_2	C_3	C_4	C_5	C_6	C_7	C_8
Piano:	C_4	C_{16}	C_{28}	C_{40}	C_{52}	C_{64}	C_{76}	C_{88}
Organ:	CCC	CC	C	c^1	c^2	c^3	c^4	
MIDI note	24	36	48	60	72	84	96	108

EXERCISES

EXERCISE 2-1 Write the note that represents the proper partial above each of the given fundamentals. The first one is completed as an example.

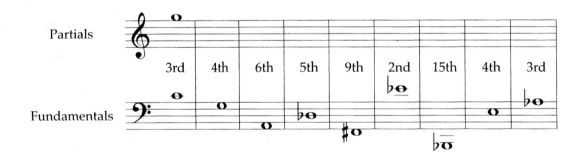

Partials

3rd   4th   6th   5th   9th   2nd   15th   4th   3rd

Fundamentals

EXERCISE 2-2 In Ex. 2-2, you will see that all of the Cs above the fundamental are part of the harmonic series. What is significant about their harmonic numbers? What is significant about the harmonic numbers of the overtones that are noticeably out of tune with the same pitches on the piano? What is the closest pitch on the piano to the 29th harmonic of Low C?

EXERCISE 2-3 Below are the beginning pitches of several well-known melodies. Name as many of them as you can, then notate them using appropriate clefs, signatures, meters, and rhythms.

Helmholtz designation: d′ d″ c♯″ a′ b′ c♯″ d″ d′ b′ a′

USA Standard designation: F$_4$ D$_5$ C$_5$ B♭$_5$ C$_5$ B♭$_5$ G$_4$ F$_4$ D$_4$

Piano key numbers: D$_{42}$ B$_{39}$ G$_{35}$ B$_{39}$ D$_{42}$ G$_{47}$ B$_{51}$ A$_{49}$ G$_{47}$ B$_{39}$ C♯$_{41}$ D$_{42}$

Organ designation: G^1 B♭^{2} C^2 D^2 E♭^{2} D^2 C^2 A^2 F^1 G^1 A^2 B♭^{2} G^1 G^1 F♯^{1} G^1

Helmholtz designation: e′ e′ f♯′ e′ a′ g♯′ e′ e′ f♯′ e′ b′ a′ e′ e′ e″

EXERCISE 2-4 Write a brief explanation why orchestras tune to A and wind ensembles tune to B♭.

****EXERCISE 2-5** A violinist tunes the A string to 440 Hz, then tunes the D string a perfect fifth below, adjusting for zero beats, then tunes the G string a fifth below the D string, also adjusting for zero beats. The piano, tuned in equal temperament, has a slightly different frequency for G below Middle C. If the piano and the violin play this pitch for five seconds, how many beats (to the nearest whole number) will there be? How did you arrive at your answer?

****EXERCISE 2-6** Suppose you wanted to tune a stringed instrument, such as a folk harp or psaltery, so that you had just tuning for the C Major scale. You could accomplish it as follows: Begin by tuning F–A–C with frequency ratio of 4–5–6, then, using the C, tune C–E–G with the 4–5–6 ratio, and finally, using the G, tune G-B-D in the same way. Now you have all of the pitches of the scale. Besides the C, F, and G major triads, you also have two minor triads, one on E and one on D. What are the advantages and disadvantages of such a tuning?

CHAPTER 3

THE NOTATION OF MUSIC

Study this little folk song arrangement, taking note of elements of notation, then consider the questions that follow it.

Example 3-1 Notation example by the author.

Ground Hog

QUESTIONS FOR DISCUSSiON

1. What is the order of musical symbols on the first staff?

2. How do we know that the flute, the voice, and the piano perform together? What do we call the group of staves that are to be performed simultaneously?

3. What musical symbols appear at the beginning of the next "line" of the music? What indications at the beginning of the music hold good (until changed by new indications)?

4. Where do you expect to find the name of the composer, arranger, or source of the music? Where do you expect to find the name of the lyricist, poet, or source of the lyrics?

5. Where is the tempo or performance style description located? To which staves does it apply? If the ensemble required a large number of staves, such as an orchestral score, would you repeat the tempo marking anywhere else?

6. Sometimes the note stems are drawn down from the note heads and sometimes up from them. Can you describe the principles that govern stem direction for the flute and voice parts?

7. A piano part normally gets two staves. Can you give reasons for this? Why does the bar line connect the piano staves together but not the others? The stems on the notes in the upper piano staff are treated differently from those of the other staves. Why?

8. What considerations govern the spacing and alignment of the notation and text? The measure rest for the flute part is treated differently from other notation elements. Why is it aligned differently? Why isn't this measure filled with two quarter rests or a half rest?

9. Where are the dynamic markings located for the flute part? the voice part? the piano part?

10. Where are the lyrics located in relation to the notes? How are words with more than one syllable indicated? How does the notation in measure 3 show that "and" is to be sung to two notes?

11. Slurs show a smooth connection between notes. In the flute and voice parts, they connect the note heads and curve in the opposite direction to the direction of the stems. Why are they treated differently in the upper staff of the piano part?

12. In measures 2 and 4 in the piano part, there are notes to be played together that are on an adjacent line and space (E and F in m. 2, G and A in m. 4). They have been offset from each other in order to avoid crowding. Which of the two notes is on the left and which on the right? The final chord shows an A and B♭ oriented differently. Can you state the governing principle?

13. Articulation symbols indicate how a note is to be played. In this example, there are staccato marks (dots), tenuto marks (dashes), and accent marks (>). How are they oriented to the notes?

PRINCIPLES AND PRACTICES

Our system of musical notation is a living symbolic language that has its roots in the past but changes to serve modern usage. The following outline describes the state of some standards of its present-day usage. This summary does not include basic information on pitch names or on time values for notes and rests (see Chapter 4 for these items). It covers score conventions of which students are often unaware, even after years of performance.

Music notation software incorporates some, but not all, of these principles. Music students should be skilled in the use of standard notation in spite of the fact that the computer can be expected to treat stems, ties, spacing, and alignment correctly. Handwritten manuscript must adhere to the same rules and practices.

A. BASIC CONVENTIONS FOR WESTERN MUSIC NOTATION SYSTEMS, PAST AND PRESENT

1. The pitch dimension is represented vertically (like the Y axis in a graph).

2. A pitch grid system—the *staff* in standard notation—is used to indicate pitch. Clef signs are used to show register (and to allow the majority of notes to be within the staff).

3. The temporal dimension is represented horizontally, from left to right (like the X axis in a graph).

4. A time grid system—*measures* in standard notation—is used to show elapsed time. Meter signs are used to organize the rhythm and pulse.

B. SUMMARY OF PRESENT STANDARD PRACTICES IN WESTERN MUSIC NOTATION

1. Global indications (left to right)

   a. Left of the staff

      i) Name of instrument or instrumental group, solo, or choral voice part. For some instruments or groups, the name is placed between staves (piano, harp, organ, marimba, violin section, and so on).
      ii) Brackets and braces. Square brackets show instrumental or choral family groupings (wood winds, strings, and so on). The curved brace shows that more than one staff is used by a single instrument (piano, harp), or a subset within a group (Violins I and II).
      iii) Left bar line. All parts that sound together in a score should be joined by a left bar line. Music for unaccompanied solo and individual parts do not need a left bar line.

   b. Required staff indications

      i) Clef. The clef should appear as the first staff indication on every part in a score and on every line or system in the score (with the exception noted in Item iv below).
      ii) Signature. If there is a signature, it should appear immediately to the right of the clef on every part in a score and on every line or system in the score.
      iii) Meter (or time signature). The meter appears after the signature (if there is one) on every part on the first system of a score. It is *not* repeated in subsequent lines or systems (except where a change of meter is needed).
      iv) In jazz and commercial notation, the clef, signature, and meter, followed by a curved line, are often given only at the beginning. Subsequent staves use only a left bar line to begin the staff.

2. Changes of signature and meter

   a. When a change of signature is required, the new signature is given in all parts. This is usually at the beginning of a measure. In older scores, the old signature is canceled with natural signs, but this practice is no longer required, except when the new signature contains no sharps or flats. If a system begins with a new signature, it must be indicated at the end of the previous system following the bar line. The bar line before a signature change is often doubled to call attention to the change.

   b. When a change of meter is required, the new meter is given in all parts. This is usually at the beginning of a measure. If a system begins with a new meter, it must be indicated at the end of the previous system following the bar line. The bar line before a meter change is normally doubled if it comes at the beginning of a new section of the music. If the music has frequent or occasional meter changes, bar lines are not doubled.

3. Spacing and alignment

   a. Notes and rests are aligned vertically at the point where they begin, with the exception of a full measure rest (see Item e below).

   b. Notes and rests are generally spaced proportionately according to their time value within a measure. For example, in common time, a half note or rest is given approximately half the length of the measure; in $\frac{3}{4}$ meter, a half note or rest is given two-thirds of the length of a measure.

   c. Notes of short duration may be given more space to avoid crowding; notes of long duration may be given less space. In vocal music, crowding of text syllables must be avoided without completely skewing the spatial relationship of the rhythm to the measure.

   d. Accidentals always precede the notes they affect (and the point where the notes begin). Extra space is given for accidentals, especially when they are used with chords and tone clusters. To avoid crowding, the lower of two accidentals is placed to the left of the higher accidental.

   e. The whole rest ≡ is used in two different ways: When centered within a measure it takes the value of a full measure of rest in the current meter. In large meters such as $\frac{3}{2}$ and $\frac{4}{2}$, it takes the value of a whole note.

4. Positioning for staves containing a single part

   a. When notes are located below the middle line of the staff, stems are drawn on the right of the note head and point up. When notes are located above the third line, stems are drawn on the left of the note heads and point down. When a note is on the middle staff line, its stem may be up or down, but it responds to the prevailing stem direction of neighboring notes.

   b. For chords and notes beamed together, stems respond to the average distance of notes from the middle line.

   c. When two notes in a chord are a second apart (on adjacent pair of lines and spaces), they must be offset in order to avoid crowding. The lower of the two notes is placed to the left of the upper note. Here are several examples of chords containing seconds:

    d. Rests are positioned in the center of the staff (with the exception of the whole rest, which hangs from the next-to-highest staff line; and the half rest, which sits on the middle staff line).

    e. Ties and slurs are drawn from the note heads and curve over for notes above the middle staff line and under for notes below the middle staff line.

    f. Notes of different durations should not be joined together with a single stem.

5. Positioning on a staff containing two parts

    a. The parts are distinguished by stem direction and rest positioning. All stems for the upper part point up, and rests are offset above the middle staff line. All stems for the lower part point down, and rests are offset below the middle staff line.

    b. When notes in the two parts begin at the same time and are a second apart, the upper part's note head is placed to the left of the note head in the lower part (see Ex. 3-1, mm 2 and 4 in the upper staff of the piano part).

    c. Rests are offset enough to avoid collision with notes and rests in the other part.

    d. Slurs are drawn next to stems and beams. They curve in the same direction as the direction of the stems.

6. Dynamics and articulations

    a. Dynamic markings for individual instrumental parts appear below the notation. If two contrapuntal parts are written in a single staff, it may be necessary to position the dynamics for the upper part above its notation.

    b. Dynamics for vocal and choral parts are written above the notation, allowing the space below the notation for the lyrics.

    c. Dynamics for instruments using two staves (such as piano), are written between the staves, unless a different marking is needed for each staff.

    d. Articulations (accents, staccato marks, tenuto marks, etc.) are generally centered above or below the note head. They may need to be positioned on the stem or beam side when two parts occupy a single staff.

    e. Trill signs and other signs for ornaments are generally placed above the notation.

7. Positioning of lyrics

    a. Each syllable should be centered beneath the note to which it is assigned.

    b. Hyphens are used between syllables of compound words.

    c. When a one-syllable word or the last syllable of a compound word is to be sung for two or more notes, a base-line is attached and extended to the last note of the melisma or group of notes assigned to that syllable. The notes in a melisma also are connected by a slur.

    d. When a melisma occurs on any syllable except the last of a compound word, one or more hyphens are centered between that and the next syllable, and the notes of the melisma are connected by a slur.

    e. The lyrics must be faithful to the punctuation and capitalization of the original text. Repeated words or phrases should be set off by commas.

EXERCISES   **EXERCISE 3-1** Rewrite this example, correcting as many notational errors as you can.

EXERCISE 3-2 Transcribe this example for piano.

EXERCISE 3-3 Rewrite in open score using the given clefs. The tenor part uses treble clef down an octave.

A - maz - ing- grace! how sweet the sound that saved a— wretch— like me!

S.

A.

T.

B.

*__EXERCISE 3-4__ Transcribe Example 1-1 for string quartet. Use alto clef for the viola.

*__EXERCISE 3-5__ Convert this sequencer graph of the beginning of a Bach Chorale to a piano score. Key: D minor. Meter: $\frac{4}{4}$.

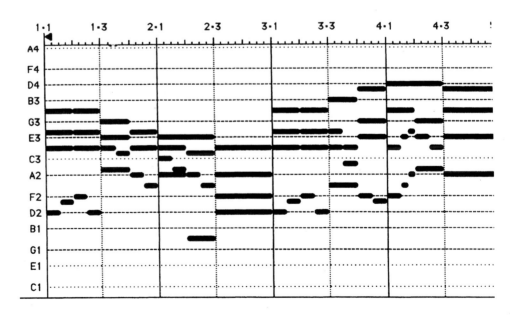

*EXERCISE 3-6 Make a piano reduction of this excerpt from a woodwind quintet. The clarinet and horn are transposed parts.

CHAPTER 4

THE TEMPORAL DIMENSION

Example 4-1 "Modern Music" by William Billings (1746–1800).

Example 4-1 (*continued*)

Example 4-1 (*continued*)

Example 4-1 (*continued*)

Example 4-2 Agnus Dei II from *Missa de Beata Virgine* by Josquin des Prez (1440–1521).

William Billings spent his whole life in Boston, Massachusetts. He was a self-taught musician, gaining what he could from the few music texts available in New England in the eighteenth century. European musicians would have considered his music simple, even somewhat "crude" (note parallel fifths in measures 62–63). The music is charming, nonetheless. With the exception of the "fuging" section, the tenor carries the melodic lead throughout. The piece is included here for its straightforward use of meters and rhythms.

Josquin des Prez, the great early Renaissance composer, often included sections for two voices in his motets and masses. Ex. 4-2 shows typical early Renaissance rhythmic complexity.

QUESTIONS FOR DISCUSSION

1. What distinguishes music from the visual arts?

2. What elements in music are concerned with time?

3. How is form in music related to temporal elements?

4. What kinds of music require a steady beat?

5. What kinds of music do not require a steady beat?

6. How is beat related to meter?

7. What is wrong with this statement: "The upper number in the time signature tells how many beats there are in the measure, and the lower number tells what kind of a note gets a beat."

8. "Modern Music" by William Billings, Ex. 4-1, has several sections, each marked off by a double bar and a change of meter. Each section has been given a metronome marking. How would you conduct each section?

9. If you were to replace the metronome markings in Ex. 4-1 with Italian tempo expressions, what would be your choices? What English tempo expressions would you choose?

10. The beat is not very strong in Ex. 4-2, but the music seems to move along with a rather steady pulse. How would you conduct it? What metronome setting would you suggest for the piece?

11. How would you define the word *rhythm?* How would you characterize the rhythms in Ex. 4-1?

12. How does the rhythmic texture of Ex. 4-2 compare to that of Ex. 4-1?

DEFINITIONS, PRINCIPLES, AND OBSERVATIONS

Music exists in the realm of time. That is the main characteristic that distinguishes music from the visual arts. Some music has a very strong and steady beat, such as rock music, marches, and most dance music. Some music has a more subtle feeling of beat, such as the nocturnes of Chopin and "new age" music. Still other music has virtually no regular pulse or beat, such as Gregorian Chant and opera recitative. Form in music unfolds in time, and we become conscious of it as we hear relationships among the parts that make up the whole of a piece. We have a general idea of what is meant by the words pulse, beat, meter, rhythm, and tempo, but the following working definitions will be useful in our summary of the temporal dimension of music.

A. DEFINITIONS

    1. *Pulse and beat.* We often use these terms interchangeably to denote a per-ceived stimulus like a series thumps or clicks, usually continuous, evenly spaced, and of equal strength. The term *beat*, however, is used specifically as a unit of *meter*. We can perceive the beat at several levels. For example, in the minimalist music of John Adams, the beat is perceived at the eighth-note level; in most rock music, the beat is at the quarter-note level; in Viennese waltzes, it is at the dotted-half note level.

    2. *Tactus.* The beat level at which we "keep time" to the music and the beat level that is best for conducting.

    3. *Tempo.* The pace or perceived speed of the music. It may be indicated in the score by descriptive words such as *allegro, adagio, fast, slow*; or it may be given as a metronome marking such as ♩ = 72 (a rate of seventy-two pulses per minute).

    4. *Meter.* The organization of the tactus into regularly recurring patterns of stresses and unstresses. The meter is specified by the *time signature.*

    5. *Rhythm.* The pattern of musical events in time. Rhythm is perceived as a con-tinuity of sounds of longer or shorter duration. Rhythm may or may not con-form to a meter.

B. MECHANICS OF METER

    1. *Grouping of the tactus.* Beats at the tactus level are usually grouped to form the *measure* or *bar*. Some measures, however, may have a single tactus. When the tactus is grouped in twos, the result is *duple meter.* Grouping the tactus in threes produces *triple meter.* Grouping in fours is called *quadruple meter*, and so on.

    2. *Division of the tactus.* Beats at the tactus level can be divided into halves or thirds. Division into halves is called *simple division*; division into thirds is called *compound division.* Beat divisions can be subdivided as well into halves or thirds.

C. TIME SIGNATURES

    1. For simple-duple meter, two beats per measure:

Signature:	¢	2/2 2/4	2/8
Tactus	𝅗𝅥	𝅗𝅥	♩	♪

    2. For simple-triple meter, three beats per measure in moderate to slow tempo:

Signature:	3/2	3/4	3/8
Tactus	𝅗𝅥	♩	♪

    In fast tempo, one beat per measure:

Signature:	3/2	3/4	3/8
Tactus	𝅝.	𝅗𝅥.	♩.

3. For simple-quadruple meter, four beats per measure:

Signature: $\frac{4}{2}$ $\mathbf{c}$ $\frac{4}{4}$ $\frac{4}{8}$

Tactus: 𝅗𝅥 ♩ ♩ ♪

4. For compound-duple meter, two beats per measure:

Signature: $\frac{6}{4}$ $\frac{6}{8}$ $\frac{6}{16}$

Tactus: 𝅗𝅥. ♩. ♪.

NOTE: There are six beats in the measure only when the tempo is very slow.

5. For compound-triple meter, three beats per measure:

Signature: $\frac{9}{4}$ $\frac{9}{8}$ $\frac{9}{16}$

Tactus: 𝅗𝅥. ♩. ♪.

6. For compound-quadruple meter, four beats per measure:

Signature: $\frac{12}{8}$ $\frac{12}{16}$

Tactus: ♩. ♪.

7. *Asymmetric meters* are those that contain beats of different lengths. Each beat may contain two or three subdivisions. The values of the subdivisions are represented by the lower number in the signature. When the upper number is 5, the pattern is usually 2 + 3 or 3 + 2—unless the tempo is slow, in which case there will be five beats. When the upper number is 7, the pattern is usually 2 + 2 + 3, 2 + 3 + 2, or 3 + 2 + 2. In signatures whose upper number is 8 or larger, there are several possible patterns of twos and threes.

8. Sometimes the signature shows the beat divisions as in this example:

$$\frac{3+2+2+3}{8}$$

9. In some contemporary scores, the signature appears like this:

$\frac{3}{\text{♩.}} \left(\text{equivalent to } \frac{9}{8} \right)$

10. In (a) below, two meters alternate throughout the piece. In (b), the meter may shift at any time from one meter to the other:

a. $\frac{2}{4} + \frac{3}{4}$ b. $\frac{3}{4} \left(\frac{6}{8} \right)$

D. SYMBOLS

1. Notes and rests

American name	English name	Note	Equivalent to	Rest
Double whole	Breve	𝄺 or 𝄺	o + o	≡
Whole	Semibreve	o	𝅗𝅥 + 𝅗𝅥	≡
Half	Minim	𝅗𝅥	♩ + ♩	≡
Quarter	Crotchet	♩	♪ + ♪	𝄽
Eighth	Quaver	♪	𝅘𝅥𝅮 + 𝅘𝅥𝅮	𝄾
Sixteenth	Semiquaver	𝅘𝅥𝅯	𝅘𝅥𝅯 + 𝅘𝅥𝅯	𝄿
Thirty-second	Demisemiquaver	𝅘𝅥𝅰	𝅘𝅥𝅰 + 𝅘𝅥𝅰	𝅀
Sixty-fourth	Hemidemisemiquaver	𝅘𝅥𝅱	𝅘𝅥𝅱 + 𝅘𝅥𝅱	𝅁

2. Dots

A dot placed to the right of a note or rest prolongs its duration by half again its value. A second dot adds half again the value of the first dot.

Dots are always placed in a space, never on a staff line.

3. The whole rest is used for the whole measure for all meters except for those whose total duration exceeds the value of a whole note.

E. BEAMS AND TIES

1. Beaming of notes facilitates music reading by showing the structure of the meter. Note in this example how beaming can distinguish compound duple meter from simple triple meter.

Example 4-3 Beamed groups.

2. A single beam may connect notes spanning more than one beat if the first note in the beam is on a beat.

Example 4-4 Beaming across beats.

3. The two halves of a measure in a meter with an even number of beats should be indicated by the beaming or by the use of ties. Beams should not cross the middle of the bar. Some permitted exceptions are noted.

Example 4-5 Showing the second half of the measure.

Third beat shows clearly

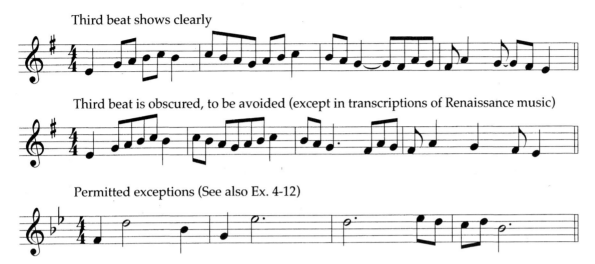

Third beat is obscured, to be avoided (except in transcriptions of Renaissance music)

Permitted exceptions (See also Ex. 4-12)

4. Beamed groups should show beats clearly in compound meter.

Example 4-6 Beaming in compound meter.

Beats show clearly.   Beats are obscured.

5. Beams are preferred to separate flags. Although older vocal notation used flags for each syllable for notes shorter than quarter notes, the modern standard is for use of beams (see Ex. 3-1).

Example 4-7 Using beams instead of flags.

Preferred   Avoid

6. Use ties for notes that are prolonged across major metrical units (from one measure to the next, across the middle of the measure in meters with an even number of beats). Avoid unnecessary ties.

Example 4-8 Using ties to show strong beats.

F. TUPLETS

    1. Tuplets are used for rhythmic groupings that do not conform to the metrical subdivisions. A triplet indicates that there will be three notes (or rests) of a given duration in the space of two. A duplet indicates two in the space of three.

    2. Tuplets may be notated in a number of ways as shown below.

Example 4-9 Tuplet notation.

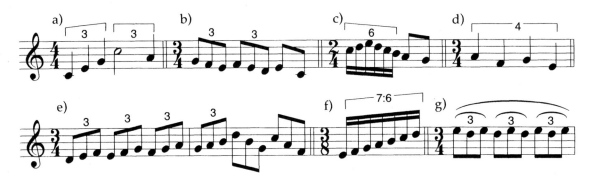

    a. Number with bracket, recommended for notes without beams.
    b. Number without bracket, useful when beams show note grouping.
    c. Number and bracket may be used with beamed notes.
    d. Number with broken bracket.
    e. The numbers may be omitted after the first few triplets when it is obvious that triplets will continue.
    f. Tuplet shown as a ratio: 7 in the space of 6.
    g. Number with slur—This older style of triplet indication is not recommended because slurs may be confused with articulation markings.

G. ANACRUSIS

    1. *Anacrusis* is the term given to one or more notes preceding the first full measure of a piece or phrase. Other terms in common use are *pick-up*, and *upbeat*. See upbeat of Ex. 4-1.

    2. When an anacrusis is short (half a measure or less), it is notated in an incomplete bar without preceding rests. The final measure is often incomplete, having only the time value that is missing from the bar occupied by the anacrusis. For example, if a minuet begins with an anacrusis of one beat, the last measure often will be just two beats long.

    3. When measure numbers are used, the anacrusis is not counted as a measure. Measure 1 is always the first full measure.

    4. When you extract parts for a piece that begins with an anacrusis, it is essential that all parts not playing the anacrusis be given equivalent rests.

H. METRIC DISPLACEMENT DEVICES. The metric flow may be interrupted or displaced in several ways. If the displacement is relatively short, no change in meter is indicated in the notation.

1. *Syncopation:* a rhythmic figure that shifts the metric stresses, often to the weak beats.

2. *Hemiola:* a rhythmic figure that substitutes a duple metric pulse with a triple one. A good example is "America," from *West Side Story* by Leonard Bernstein.

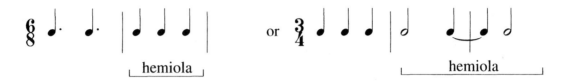

3. *Cross rhythm:* a rhythmic pattern that goes against the prevailing meter (see Ex. 4-12).

I.   SOME SPECIAL CASES

1. Rests may be included in beamed groups; half stems may be used with rests.

Example 4-10 Rests within beamed groups.

2. Feathered beams may be used to show gradual decreases or increases in note durations.

Example 4-11 Feathered beams.

3. Cross rhythms are often beamed in a way that shows the rhythmic pattern clearly.

Example 4-12 Notation of cross rhythms.

4. Music of the Renaissance is sometimes notated in a way that shows the flow of the polyphonic lines. Note in the example below, based on the opening of Ex. 4-2, that notes are given their full value without using ties. A reference bar line, called a *Mensurstrick*, appears between, rather than on, the staves. The meter here signifies that the half note gets the beat.

Example 4-13 Notation of Renaissance music.

Josquin des Prez

EXERCISES

EXERCISE 4-1 Continue the notation of these familiar tunes.

EXERCISE 4-2 Rewrite with correct use of beams and ties.

EXERCISE 4-3 What is wrong with the notation of these familiar tunes? Rewrite them correctly.

***EXERCISE 4-4** Notate this rhythmic sequence:

a. in simple duple meter.

b. in compound duple meter.

c. in simple triple meter.

***EXERCISE 4-5** Using Ex. 4-13 as a beginning, complete a new version of Ex. 4-2. Give special attention to vertical alignment.

CHAPTER 5

THE PITCH DIMENSION

The melodies in Ex. 5-1 are taken from a variety of sources. They exhibit the qualities of different modes and scales. They also show various treatments of tonality. All have been notated without signatures. Sing or play them, then discuss the questions that follow.

Example 5-1 Melodies for discussion.

Example 5-1 (*continued*)

g. Symphony (first movement)　　　　　　　　　　　　　　　　　　　C. Franck

h. Pange lingua gloriosi　　　　　　　　　　　　　　　　　　　Gregorian hymn

i. Vivace　　　　　　　　　　　　　　　　　　　　　　　　　(by the Author)

j. God rest ye merry, gentlemen　　　　　　　　　　　　　　　　English carol

k. Oi, Tate　　　　　　　　　　　　　　　　　　　　　　　　　Klezmer

l. Mäßig schnell　　　　　　　　　　　　　　　　　　　　　(by the Author)

m. Gently, Johnny my jingalo　　　　　　　　　　　　　　　　　Scottish

n. Sonata, Op. 2, No. 2 (third movement)　　　　　　　　　　　　Beethoven

Example 5-1 (*continued*)

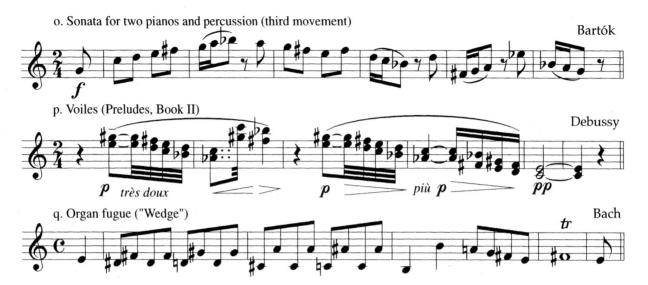

o. Sonata for two pianos and percussion (third movement)

Bartók

p. Voiles (Preludes, Book II)

Debussy

p *très doux* *p* *più p* *pp*

q. Organ fugue ("Wedge")

Bach

QUESTIONS FOR DISCUSSION

1. Can you tell which tone in each of the melodies is DO? Do any of these melodies seem to have *no* tones that you perceive as DO? Does DO seem to shift from one location to another in any of the melodies? Do any of the melodies seem to have two tones that could be DO?

2. How do we perceive a tone as DO? Are there any ways we can predict DO just from looking at the music?

3. Which of the melodies would you consider to be *diatonic*? Which would you describe as *chromatic*? Which seem to *modulate* or change key?

4. Key signatures have not been used for any of the melodies. What signatures would you consider the best choice for each of the melodies?

5. Which of the melodies are in the major? in some kind of minor? in one of the so-called *church modes?* Which appear to be made up of pitches that do not belong to any of the above?

DEFINITIONS, PRINCIPLES, AND OBSERVATIONS

This chapter explores the way pitch is organized by tonality, pitch naming, scales and modes, clefs, signatures, and intervals in Western music (see Chapter 18 for a discussion of the pitch dimension in non-Western musics). The most fundamental information is not included here, since that is the task of a basic theory text. What is presented should provide a larger context for your consideration.

A. TONALITY. Music can be described as *tonal, nontonal* (or *atonal*), *modal, diatonic,* or *chromatic.* These terms describe the nature of the relationships among the pitches in a piece of music.

   1. In *tonal* music, the pitches exhibit a relationship to a *tonal center* or *tonic.* The tonic exerts an attraction on the other pitches not unlike the sun for the planets in the solar system. Music in major, minor, and various modes is considered to be tonal (with the exception noted in Item 4 below).

2. The word *mode* is often used in a general way, having the same meaning as *scale*. When used in this way, major and minor are considered modes.

3. The *church modes* or *ecclesiastical modes* are the *Dorian, Phrygian, Lydian, Mixolydian, Aeolian* (which is equivalent to the Natural Minor), and the *Ionian* (equivalent to the major). The *Locrian* also is included occasionally, but it is rarely encountered in music and is not one of the church modes.

4. The term *modal* (the adjective form) is applied to music that exhibits characteristics of various modes (church modes and other modes), excluding major and minor. When *modal* and *tonal* are used together, *tonal* refers to major and minor only.

5. Music in which there is no tonic is referred to as *nontonal* or *atonal*. The term *pantonal* was used by Arnold Schoenberg to describe music in which all pitches have an equal focus. *Serial music* and *twelve-tone music* are terms applied to music organized by pitch-class series, rather than by scales or modes. This music is explored in Chapter 19.

6. Some music is strongly tonal at times, but at other times the tonal center is vague, obscured, or lacking. A useful way to describe this music is "varying in tonal focus."

7. Some music has two or more tonal centers active simultaneously. The terms *bitonal* and *polytonal* are used to describe this kind of music (see Ex. 19-5).

8. Music is considered *diatonic* if most of its pitches belong to the major, minor, or one of the modes containing no more than seven scale degrees.

9. Music is considered *chromatic* if it makes liberal use of tones of the chromatic scale or collection.

10. Tonal music may be diatonic or chromatic depending upon the degree to which tones outside of the prevailing mode are employed.

B. PITCH NAMING AND NOTATION. As a music major, you know the fundamentals of pitch naming and reading pitches in one or two clefs. You can probably name the keys on the piano. Some of the following information will not be new to you, but some terms and concepts will be unfamiliar and are important to the well-educated musician.

1. The letters A through G are used to name the pitches corresponding to the white keys on the piano. The letter H is used by German musicians for our B-natural. The letter B is used by German musicians for our B-flat.

2. Pitches corresponding to the black keys on the piano are indicated by a sharp or flat added to the letter name of the adjacent white key. The sharp is used to designate the key immediately to the right of a white key (F♯ is to the right of F; B♯ is to the right of B). The flat is used to designate a key immediately to the left of a white key (G♭ is to the left of G, C♭ is left of C).

3. Looking at the piano keyboard you can see that the black keys can be named either as a sharp or a flat. Alternate names for the same pitch are called *enharmonic equivalents*. For example: F♯ = G♭, B♭ = A♯, E = F♭, B♯ = C, F𝄪 = G, A = B♭♭.

4. *Pitch class* denotes all pitches with the same name, regardless of register or octave placement (all the Es on the piano are pitch class E). Enharmonic equivalent pitches denote a single pitch class. Pitch class can be designated by letter name or by number as shown below.

PITCH CLASS NOMENCLATURE

Name	C	C♯/D♭	D	D♯/E♭	E	F	F♯/G♭	G	G♯/A♭	A	A♯/B♭	B
Number	0	1	2	3	4	5	6	7	8	9	10	11

5. MIDI code does not differentiate between enharmonic equivalent pitches. For example: F♯ above Middle C is MIDI note 66. G♭ above Middle C is also MIDI note 66.

C. SCALE STRUCTURES. A scale is a representation of the available pitches in any mode (used here in its general sense) or pitch collection arranged in ascending order. The Melodic Minor is represented both ascending and descending due to the manner in which it is used.

1. *Solfège* or the *sol-fa* syllable system is used as an aid in identifying and expressing the aural quality of the various scale degrees. We use DO to represent the tonic of all scales (major, minor, and all other modes). This system is known as *moveable do*, since the tonic can be on any pitch (depending on the "key" or transposition from C as tonic). Some European musicians use *fixed do*, where do = C, di = C♯, re = D, ri = D♯, mi = E, and so on, no matter where the tonic resides. This system is useful for singing and hearing atonal music. Another commonly used system uses the major for reference, beginning the minor on LA.

2. Scale degrees are identified by careted numbers and by names as shown below.

$\hat{1}$	$\hat{2}$	$\hat{3}$	$\hat{4}$	$\hat{5}$	$\hat{6}$	$\hat{7}$
Tonic	Supertonic	Mediant	Subdominant	Dominant	Submediant	Leading tone

3. Scale forms differ from one another according to the order of whole and half steps.

STEP PATTERNS FOR VARIOUS SCALES

Scale name	Scale degrees. Each square represents a half step.												
Chromatic	1	2	3	4	5	6	7	8	9	10	11	12	1
Major	1		2		3	4		5		6		7	1
Dorian	1		2	3		4		5		6	7		1
Phrygian	1	2		3		4		5	6		7		1
Lydian	1		2		3		4	5		6		7	1
Mixolydian	1		2		3	4		5		6	7		1
Aeolian	1		2	3		4		5	6		7		1
Locrian	1	2		3		4	5		6		7		1
Harmonic Minor	1		2	3		4		5	6			7	1
Whole-tone	1		2		3		4		5		6		1
Octatonic	1		2	3		4	5		6	7		8	1

4. *Gapped scale* designates scales that contain one or more gaps wider than a whole step (such as the Harmonic Minor).

5. Before the middle of the seventeenth century, the church modes were designated by number, rather than the Greek names we use today. The following are rough equivalents: Modes I and II are Dorian, III and IV are Phrygian, V and VI are Lydian, VII and VIII are Mixolydian.

6. The *chromatic scale* includes all twelve pitches within the octave in equal temperament.

7. The *whole tone scale* is a series of ascending whole steps.

8. The *octatonic scale* is an alternation of whole and half steps, beginning with a whole step (as shown above) or a half step. It is called the *diminished scale* by jazz musicians.

9. The term *pitch collection* is used to describe an unordered group of pitches, in contrast to a scale, which is an ordered group of pitches.

The chart below shows the most common scale structures beginning on C with the proper sol-fa syllables for each scale degree.

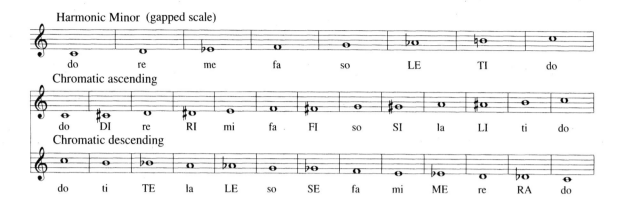

Notes on the Scale Structures Chart

1. *Sol-fa* syllables appear beneath each note of every scale. The fifth degree syllable "sol" has been given simply as "so" for the following reasons: a) to agree with all others, which are spelled with two letters, the second being a vowel; b) "so" is much easier to sing, especially in quick tempo; and c) the "o" sound is shared by "do," indicating the special nature of the tonic and the dominant scale degrees.

2. Syllables that carry special modal significance are printed IN UPPER CASE. The church modes can be conveniently described as follows: Lydian is Major with FI (rather than FA), Mixolydian is Major with TE, Dorian is [Natural] Minor with LA, Phrygian is Minor with RA.

3. The first three scales can be referred to as "Proto-Major," since they all have MI as their third degree. Add one sharp to (or take one flat from) any Major scale to produce the Lydian. Add one flat to (or take one sharp from) any Major scale to produce the Mixolydian.

4. The next three scales can be referred to as "Proto-Minor," since they all have ME (pronounced "may") as their third degree. Add one sharp to (or take one flat from) any Minor scale to produce the Dorian. Add one flat to (or take one sharp from) any Minor scale to produce the Phrygian.

Proto-Major Modes			Proto-minor Modes		
Lydian L	Ionian I	Mixolydian M	Dorian D	Aeolian A	Phrygian P
+ 1 sharp or −1 flat	Start	−1 sharp or + 1 flat	+ 1 sharp or −1 flat	Start	−1 sharp or + 1 flat

5. The Locrian mode is seldom used, because of its lowered fifth degree (which produces a tritone with the tonic). It is included, however, for the sake of completeness. A scale on white keys only from B through the octave is Locrian.

6. Note that if signatures were used for the scales from the Lydian down through the Locrian, they would appear to be those for Major keys of G, C, F, B♭, E♭, A♭, and D♭, moving backwards through the Circle of Fifths.

7. The Melodic Minor uses LA-TI as it ascends toward DO and TE-LE as it descends toward SO.

8. The Harmonic Minor consists of the tones that comprise the Primary Triads in a minor key (i–iv–V). The interval from LE to TI is an augmented second, perceived as a "gap." This scale is rarely found in Western music as a resource for melody.

9. The members of the tonic triad in most scales (DO, MI or ME, SO) are generally considered to be "stable tones"—tones that are the goal of melodic motion. The other tones are generally considered to be "active tones"—tones that call for melodic motion (TI-do, FA-mi, LA-so, RE-do, and so on).

10. Active tones with syllables ending in "i" (sounding "ee") have an upward tendency (TI-do, FI-so, and so on). Active tones with syllables ending in "e" (sounding "ay" as in "play") or "a" (sounding "ah") have a downward tendency (LE-so, RA-do, and so on). Syllables ending in "o" (sounding "oh") are used only by DO and SO, the tonic and dominant tones.

D. CLEFS. You are undoubtedly familiar with the basic principles of notating and reading in treble and bass clef. Here are some facts that you may not know that will be useful to you as you become a skilled musician.

1. Choice of clef is determined by instrument or voice type. For instruments with a large range, a choice of clefs is available. The proper clef is chosen in order to allow as many notes as possible to be within the staff.

2. Treble clef, which positions G above middle C on the second line, is used by the flute family, the oboe and English horn, the clarinet family, the saxophone family, all sizes of trumpets and cornets, French horn (except for its lowest range), all of the higher pitched percussion instruments, the violin, and female voices. Keyboard instruments, harp, marimba, viola and cello use it for their upper ranges. The piccolo uses the treble clef, but the pitches are actually an octave higher than written. For some of the very high-pitched percussion instruments, the pitches are two octaves above where written.

3. Alto clef, which positions middle C on the third line, is used by the viola. In music printed before the twentieth century, it was often used for the trombone and the alto voice and occasionally for the left-hand part for organ music.

4. The tenor clef, which positions middle C on the fourth line, is used by the bassoon and the cello when the music is largely in the range of the tenor voice. The trombone often uses the tenor clef in solo and orchestral music when it is in its high register. In music printed before the twentieth century, the tenor clef was often used for the tenor voice.

5. Bass clef, which positions F below middle C on the fourth line, is used by the bassoon, the trombone, the euphonium, the timpani, baritone and bass voices, and the lower ranges of keyboard instruments, harp, and cello. The contrabassoon and the string bass use the bass clef, but the pitches are actually an octave lower than written. The French horn uses the bass clef for its lowest register, and occasionally the bass clarinet part is written in bass clef. With the exception of the French horn, parts for bass clef instruments are nontransposing.

6. Clefs with superscript and subscript octave signs are becoming more and more used to show that the notes on the staff sound an octave higher or lower than written. The tenor voice uses the treble clef with an 8 below it almost universally. The soprano recorder often uses the treble clef with an 8 above it. The bass recorder often uses a bass clef with an 8 above it. Some guitar music uses treble clef with an 8 below it.

7. The *grand staff* is a pair of staves connected by a curved brace and is used for piano and other keyboard instruments, harp, marimba and vibraphone (although simple marimba and vibraphone parts may appear on a single staff). Below is a grand staff showing the five most common clefs, each showing Middle C.

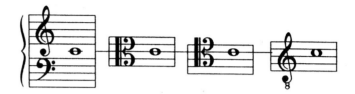

8. When a clef change occurs at the beginning of a measure, the new clef is placed just ahead of the bar line, and the clef is drawn in miniature (about seventy-five percent). If a system begins with a different clef, the new clef must appear just ahead of the bar line at the end of the previous system. A mid-measure clef change also uses a miniature clef sign. Spaces should be left in other staves in the system in vertical alignment with any clef changes.

E. SIGNATURES. The signatures for all major and minor keys are given in any theory or music fundamentals book, usually showing the Circle of Fifths. Not all sources give the following information.

   1. The order and placement of sharps and flats for treble, alto, tenor, and bass clefs are shown below.

   2. Signatures for modal music can be given in three different ways.

      a. The signature of the major or minor key that shares the same tonic may be used. Lydian and Mixolydian will use the signature of the tonic major. Dorian, Aeolian, and Phrygian will use the signature of the tonic minor. Accidentals call attention to the scale degrees that give the mode its quality.

      b. The signature of the relative major may be used. For example, Dorian on G will have one flat for its signature; Lydian on A will have four sharps for its signature.

      c. No signature may be given, and accidentals will appear where necessary. For example, Aeolian on D will have no signature, but all Bs will be flatted; Mixolydian on D will have a sharp on all Fs.

   3. Music with a rapidly changing tonal center, music whose tonal center is vague or obscure, polytonal music, and nontonal music normally use no signature.

4. Signature changes are given at the beginning of the bar where the change is to take place. It is not necessary to cancel the old signature before giving the new one unless the change is to a signature of no flats or sharps. When a system begins in a new key, the new signature must appear at the end of the previous system on a piece of the staff following the bar line.

F. INTERVALS. Below is a summary of the nomenclature and mechanics of intervals.

1. An interval is the distance between two pitches. A harmonic interval is the distance between two pitches sounding together. A melodic interval is the distance between pitches sounded successively.

2. Intervals can be named in two ways: a) by quality and size, or b) by the total number of half steps they contain. For example: the interval from E up to A is a perfect fourth. It is also "interval 5" (A is five half steps above E).

3. Interval *size* is the distance between letter names (including the lowest and highest). For example: D up to B is a sixth (six letter names—D E F G A B).

4. Intervals found within the first four pitches of the harmonic series are *perfect* intervals: the unison or prime, the fourth, the fifth, and the octave. These intervals are contained in both major and minor: Scale degrees 1 to 4 comprise a perfect fourth, 1 to 5 a perfect fifth, 1 to 8 a perfect octave.

5. Intervals in the major scale from degrees 1 to 2, 1 to 3, 1 to 6, and 1 to 7 are *major* intervals.

6. The diatonic half step and intervals in the minor scale from degrees 1 to 3, 1 to 6 and 1 to 7 are *minor* intervals.

7. The diagram below shows how expanding or contracting intervals by half steps (without changing the letter names) affects the interval quality.

← smaller			larger →
	Perfect		
Diminished	**Minor**	**Major**	**Augmented**

Interval Chart

In the chart on the next page, the symbols for the quality of intervals are given as " +, P, M, m, and °." Quality also may be indicated as "Aug., Per., Maj., Min., and Dim." For the closest harmonic ratios, only the first sixteen harmonics are used. Ratios given in parentheses are noticeably out of tune with the tempered intervals.

7. *Inversions.* Moving the lower note of an interval up an octave (or moving the upper note down an octave) produces that interval's inversion as shown in the right-most column in the Interval Chart above. Note that when intervals are inverted:

Primes become octaves; octaves become primes

Seconds become sevenths; sevenths become seconds

Thirds become sixths; sixths become thirds

Fourths become fifths, fifths become fourths
Major becomes minor; minor becomes major
Diminished becomes augmented; augmented becomes diminished
Perfect remains perfect

Name (Quality and Size)	Symbol	Example (built on C)	Alternate names	Closest Harmonic Ratio	Interval Size in Semitones	Inversion
Perfect prime	P1	C-C	unison	1 : 1	0	P 8
Augmented prime	+1	C-C♯	half step, semitone	16 : 15	1	°8
Diminished second	°2	C-D♭♭		1 : 1	0	+7
Minor second	m2	C-D♭	half step, semitone	16 : 15	1	M7
Major second	M2	C-D	whole step, tone	9 : 8	2	m7
Augmented second	+2	C-D♯		6 : 5	3	°7
Diminished third	°3	C-E♭♭		9 : 8	2	+6
Minor third	m3	C-E♭		6 : 5	3	M6
Major third	M3	C-E	tierce	5 : 4	4	m6
Augmented third	+3	C-E♯		4 : 3	5	°6
Diminished fourth	°4	C-F♭		5 : 4	4	+5
Perfect fourth	P4	C-F	diatessaron	4 : 3	5	P5
Augmented fourth	+4	C-F♯	tritone	(10 : 7)	6	°5
Diminished fifth	°5	C-G♭	tritone	(10 : 7)	6	+4
Perfect fifth	P5	C-G	diapente	3 : 2	7	P4
Augmented fifth	+5	C-G♯		8 : 5	8	°4
Diminished sixth	°6	C-A♭♭		3 : 2	7	+3
Minor sixth	m6	C-A♭		8 : 5	8	M3
Major sixth	M6	C-A		5 : 3	9	m3
Augmented sixth	+6	C-A♯		(7 : 4)	10	°3
Diminished seventh	°7	C-B♭♭		5 : 3	9	+2
Minor seventh	m7	C-B♭		16 : 9	10	M2
Major seventh	M7	C-B		15 : 8	11	m2
Augmented seventh	+7	C-B♯		2 : 1	12	°2
Diminished octave	°8	C-C♭ 8va		15 : 8	11	+1
Perfect octave	P8	C-C 8va	octave, diapason	2 : 1	12	P1

8. *Interval class.* The interval size in semitones and its inversion.

Interval class 0 = P1 and P8
Interval class 1 = m2 and M7
Interval class 2 = M2, m7, °3, and $^+$6
Interval class 3 = m3, M6, $^+$2, and °7
Interval class 4 = M3 and m6
Interval class 5 = P4 and P5
Interval class 6 = $^+$4 and °5 (tritone)

G. NONTONAL PITCH ORGANIZATION. When the tonal focus is weak, vague, obscured, or completely lacking, the pitches have no diatonic relationship to one another. In nontonal music, the pitches may be organized by the following:

1. A distinct pitch collection. Some examples are: whole-tone music, music using the octatonic pitch collection, microtonal music (employing intervals smaller than a half step).

2. Special interval sets used for melodic and harmonic structures.

3. Serial music (where order of pitches replaces diatonic orientation in tonal music).

4. Aleatory (chance operation such as random numbers, roll of dice, and so on).

EXERCISES

Several of these exercises involve familiar tunes. If you do not know some of the tunes, have someone sing them for you so that you can notate them.

EXERCISE 5-1 Name each of these tunes that have been given in solfège. A $^+$ indicates an upward move, a $^-$ indicates a downward move.

a. do, do, do, $^-$ so, $^+$ mi, mi, mi, $^-$ do, do, $^+$ mi, $^+$ so, so, $^-$ fa, $^-$ mi, re

b. so, $^+$ mi, $^-$ re, $^-$ do, $^+$ re, $^-$ do, $^-$ la, $^-$ so, $^-$ mi

c. so, so, so, so, $^-$ fa, $^-$ mi, $^+$ so, $^+$ do, $^+$ re, $^+$ mi, mi, mi, $^-$ re, do

EXERCISE 5-2 Name these tunes that have been rendered in pitch class numbers. The + and − show movement up or down. Notate them, choosing a different clef for each. In each case, use the proper signature and meter and notate the rhythm carefully. Be careful of note spelling in tune c.

a. 7, 7, $^-$2, $^+$7, $^+$9, $^-$2, $^+$11, $^-$9, $^+$11, $^+$0, $^-$11, $^-$9, $^-$7, 7, $^-$6, $^-$4, $^+$6, $^+$7, $^+$9, $^+$11, $^-$6, $^-$4, $^-$2, 2

b. 2, 2, $^+$6, $^-$3, $^-$2, $^+$6, 6, $^+$9, $^-$7, $^-$6, $^+$7, 7, $^+$10, $^-$9, $^-$7, $^-$6, $^-$3, $^-$2, $^+$3, $^+$6

c. 1, $^+$2, $^-$1, $^-$0, $^+$1, $^+$2, $^+$3, $^+$4, $^+$6, $^+$8, $^+$9, $^+$11, $^-$9, $^-$8, $^-$6, $^-$4

EXERCISE 5-3 Write these tunes in solfège (as far as there are words given). Then choose a different key for each and write the proper pitch class numbers below the sol-fa syllables.

a. Oh where, oh where has my little dog gone? Oh where, oh where can he be?

b. O beautiful for spacious skies, for amber waves of grain; for purple-mountain majesties above the fruited plain!

c. Rock-a-bye baby on the tree top. When the wind blows, the cradle will rock.

EXERCISE 5-4 Rewrite this tune up a perfect fourth and change its mode to Phrygian by entering the proper accidentals.

*EXERCISE 5-5 Rewrite this tune in E♭ Major in treble clef.

*EXERCISE 5-6 Write these tunes (at least eight measures each) with D as *do*. Use a proper signature, and identify the mode for each:

a. Greensleeves (What child is this)

b. Frère Jaques (Are you sleeping, are you sleeping, Brother John, Brother John?)

c. Kings of Orient (We three kings of Orient are)

*EXERCISE 5-7. The expression "$C2_0$" represents a pitch collection consisting of consecutive major seconds, the whole-tone scale, beginning on C. What do each of the following expressions represent?

a. $C1_0$ b. $C2_1$ c. $C3_2$ d. $C1,2_1$ e. $C4_3$

*EXERCISE 5-8 Compose a melody of about eight measures in a mode consisting of *do, re, mi, fi, so, la,* and *te*. Use tenor clef.

CHAPTER 6

THE STRUCTURAL DIMENSION
Characteristics of Melody

Example 6-1 *Tema* from Sonata in A Major, K 331, First Movement, by W. A. Mozart (1756–1791).

Example 6-2 Greek Dance Song from Zalongo.

QUESTIONS FOR DISCUSSION

1. What is melody? Write down your own definition and compare it with definitions in a few music dictionaries and encyclopedias.

2. Describe the shapes or contours of the melodies in Ex. 6-1, Ex. 6-2, and Ex. 5-1. What shapes are most common? What shapes do you feel would make poor melodies?

3. How are the melodies in Ex. 6-1 and Ex. 6-2 organized? What gives them unity or coherence? What gives them variety?

4. What is a phrase? a cadence? a motive? a sequence?

5. Which notes in Ex. 6-1 are structurally important (those that create the skeleton for the melody)? Which notes are decorative (those that give the melody character)?

6. What harmonic implications can you find in these melodies?

7. How do repetition, variation, and contrast function in these melodies to give them a coherent form or structure?

DEFINITIONS, PRINCIPLES, AND OBSERVATIONS

A. DEFINITIONS

1. *Melody.* Although the concept of melody differs from one era to another and from one culture to another, it is safe to say that melody is a *coherent succession of musical tones.* Pitches (tones) are sounded one after another (in succession), and they are perceived as "belonging together" (are coherent).

2. *Range.* The distance from the lowest to the highest notes in a melody.

3. *Tessitura.* The part of the range where most of the melody lies.

4. *Conjunct, disjunct.* These terms describe melodic motion. Conjunct motion is stepwise; disjunct motion is leapwise or skipwise.

5. *Cadence.* A point in a melody where there is a feeling of pause or conclusion. Various types of cadences are as follows:

   a. A *conclusive* or *full cadence* denotes a feeling of conclusion or pause in melodic motion, most often ending on the tonic or mediant.
   b. An *inconclusive* or *half cadence* denotes a temporary pause that suggests continuation, ending on tones other than the tonic or mediant.
   c. A *regional cadence* denotes a feeling of conclusion on a tone that functions as a "new tonic." It is most often prepared by its own leading tone.

6. *Phrase.* A relatively complete musical idea ending with some kind of cadence. A portion of a phrase that does not end with a cadence is called a *phrase member* or *subphrase.*

7. *Motive.* The smallest unit of music that has enough character to be subsequently developed. The character may be generated by the pitch contour, the rhythm, or a combination of the two.

8. *Repetition.* The reiteration of a musical idea without any changes. A *varied repetition* is a reiteration with some changes such as a shift up or down an octave, added tones, deleted tones, rhythmic or pitch changes that nonetheless sustain the identity of the original idea.

9. *Sequence.* The repetition of a melodic unit (motive or phrase) at one or more different pitch levels. A *tonal sequence* proceeds in a diatonic fashion; a *real sequence* is transposed exactly, effecting a modulation with each repetition.

10. *Extension.* A musical unit that has been added to a phrase, thereby extending it beyond normal expectation.

11. *Melodic inversion.* The mirror image of a melodic unit produced by intervallic motion in the opposite direction from the original.

Example 6-3 Thematic organization of Ex. 6-1.

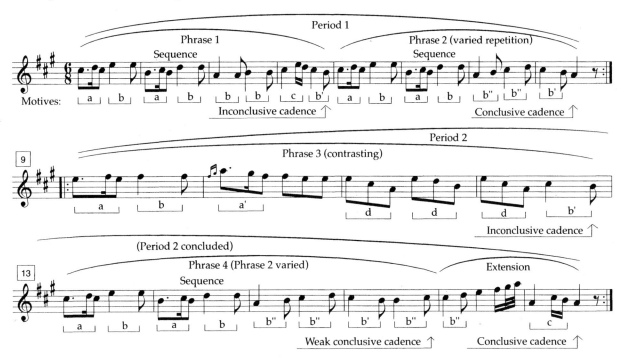

B. MELODIC CONTOUR IN WESTERN MUSIC

1. The melodic contour is the overall pitch shape of a melody.

2. Melodies are commonly wave-shaped or undulating. Other common melodic contours are arch-like, ascending, or descending shapes.

3. Conjunct motion usually predominates over disjunct motion.

4. Examples of poor melodic contours are those that are static or extremely limited in range, those with extreme range, and those that reach the highest note too often.

C. UNIFYING AND DIVERSIFYING ELEMENTS

1. Good melodies exhibit a balance of unifying and diversifying elements. An overabundance of unifying elements tends to produce a dull or boring melody. Too much diversity produces a chaotic or incoherent melody.

2. Unifying elements include repetition, sequence, and a limited number of motives.

3. Diversifying elements include contrast of musical ideas, cadence types, variation, tessitura, and tension and release (especially building to a climax and relaxation at the final cadence).

D. COMMON MELODIC STRUCTURES

1. A *large phrase* composed of a few simple patterns, having no clear internal cadences, and often making extensive use of sequences. This type of melody is more commonly found in the Baroque era than any other period of music. A good example is the opening melody in the D Minor Concerto for Harpsichord and Orchestra by J. S. Bach, BWV 1052.

2. A *repeated phrase.* Some simple melodies consist of a phrase that ends with a conclusive cadence and then is simply repeated. Example: the first two phrases of "Good King Wenceslas."

3. A *phrase chain.* Two contrasting yet compatible phrases, the second of which ends with an inconclusive cadence.

4. A *phrase group.* Two similar phrases, the second of which ends with an inconclusive cadence. Example: the first two phrases of "America the Beautiful."

5. *Period.* Two or more phrases that form a cohesive unit, with the last phrase ending in a more conclusive cadence than any that precede it. Example: "Simple Gifts" (see Ex. 5-1 c).

6. *Simple binary structure.* Two differing but compatible musical ideas presented in succession. Scheme: A-B (A and B are periods that may or may not be repeated).

7. *Rounded binary structure.* Like the simple binary, except that the final phrase brings back musical ideas presented in the first period. Scheme: A-BA (A is the first period, BA begins with a contrasting phrase and ends with a phrase resembling A).

8. *Simple ternary structure.* Two musical ideas are presented, after which the first is repeated. Scheme: A-B-A (normally three periods).

E. STRUCTURE AND TONALITY

1. Tonality often plays an important role in articulating the structure in small forms.

2. Some phrases in simple binary, rounded binary, and ternary structures may cadence to or establish a different key from the opening key. Some examples are "We three kings," "Funiculi, funicula," "The blue bells of Scotland," "Greensleeves," and "Jeanie with the light brown hair."

3. In larger forms the key-scheme is an essential ingredient in the delineation of formal units (see Chapter 14).

F. BASIC AND DECORATIVE PITCHES

1. Some tones in a melody have structural significance and will be referred to as *basic pitches.* Others provide character and will be called *decorative pitches.* Basic pitches may be found on both active and stable degrees of the scale. Those on active degrees give a feeling of forward motion or a sense of climax; basic pitches at the close of conclusive cadences are on passive scale degrees.

2. Basic pitches are likely to be found on strong beats, at turning points in the melody, and at cadence points. Longer tones are more likely than shorter tones to be basic pitches. A basic pitch may be prepared for and expected as a natural result of the preceding basic pitches.

3. Decorative pitches embellish the basic pitches. Two types are encountered:

    a. *Harmonic reinforcement tones.* These tones have a consonant or harmonic relationship with a basic pitch. These are also sometimes called *associated tones.*

    b. *Complementary tones*: tones that add decorative color or make a smooth connection to the next basic pitch. When viewed in a harmonic context, these tones are called *nonharmonic tones* or *nonchord tones*. Various types of these are shown in Ex. 6-4.

The table below describes each of the types of complementary tones.

TYPES OF COMPLEMENTARY TONES

Symbol	Name	Pitch pattern	Metric character
P	Passing tone	Approached and left in one direction by step.	Usually unaccented but occasionally accented
N	Neighbor tone or auxiliary tone	A step above or below two tones of the same pitch.	Usually unaccented but occasionally accented
DN	Double-neighbor or Neighbor Group	Two different neighbor tones between two tones of the same pitch; upper or lower may appear first.	Unaccented
E	Escape tone or Échappé	A step above the preceding tone and a third (or sometimes larger interval) above the tone that follows it. In rare cases the figure is inverted.	Unaccented
CAMB	Cambiata or Changing Tone	The four-note figure proceeds down a step, down a third, up a step. Any tone but the first may be nonharmonic.	Usually unaccented
S	Suspension	The figure consists of a basic pitch which prepares for its being suspended, then resolves down by step to the next basic pitch.	The suspension proper occurs on a strong beat.
R	Retardation	Like the suspension except that it resolves up.	The retardation proper occurs on a strong beat
L	Leaning tone or appoggiatura	Usually approached by leap, resolves down (occasionally up) by step.	Usually accented but occasionally unaccented
A	Anticipation	Anticipates a basic pitch by sounding it before it is expected.	Unaccented

Example 6-4 Types of complementary tones.

Example 6-5 Basic and decorative pitches in Ex. 6-2.

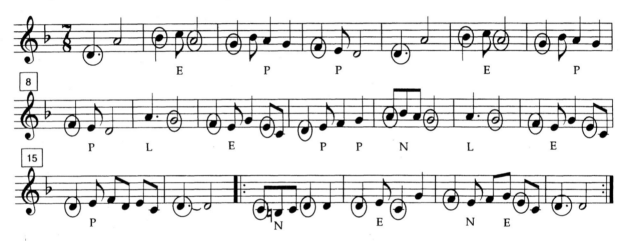

Basic pitches have been circled. Complementary tones are indicated by type. Harmonic reinforcement tones are unmarked.

4. The role of melodic tones is affected when the melody appears in a harmonic context (given a harmonic accompaniment). Basic pitches and harmonic reinforcement tones are then members of the current harmony (chord members). Complementary tones are then referred to as nonharmonic tones.

5. Complementary tones can be altered chromatically to add color to a melody. Ex. 6-6 shows the familiar chorale melody from Bach's "Jesu, joy of man's desiring," with a variation that makes liberal use of chromatic nonharmonic tones, which have been indicated by type.

Example 6-6 Chromatic nonharmonic tones.

Chorale: Werde munter, mein Gemüte

G. MELODIC REDUCTION AND ELABORATION

1. *Basic melody* is a term that describes a melody that has been reduced to its basic pitches.

2. Melodic elaboration and variation can occur with the addition of complementary tones, such as passing and neighbor tones, appoggiaturas, and so forth, and harmonic reinforcement tones, such as arpeggios.

3. Some other techniques of melodic variation are change in meter, change in mode, register changes, inversion, and changes in rhythmic figures.

Example 6-7 Melodic reduction and elaboration.

a) Original melody   b) Reduction to basic melody   c) New melodic elaboration

EXERCISES

EXERCISE 6-1 Name a few songs that have a) an arch-like contour, b) an undulating or wave-like contour, c) a descending contour, d) an ascending contour.

EXERCISE 6-2 On a copy of Ex. 6-7, identify all of the complementary tones.

EXERCISE 6-3 Using Ex. 6-3 as a model, show the thematic organization of Ex. 6-2.

EXERCISE 6-4 Using Ex. 6-5 as a model, indicate the basic and decorative pitches of Ex. 6-1.

EXERCISE 6-5 Measures 1-4 of the right-hand part of the first variation on the theme presented in Ex. 6-1 is given below. Describe in a paragraph or two how Mozart has varied the theme.

*EXERCISE 6-6 Reduce the following to basic melody (one note per bar), then compose a variation on it using a different meter.

*EXERCISE 6-7 Write a variation on "America" ("My country, 'tis of thee") in F Minor using $\frac{9}{8}$ meter.

CHAPTER 7

THE ANATOMY OF CHORDS

Example 7-1 Sarabande from *Pour le piano* by Claude Debussy (1862–1918).

Example 7-1 (*continued*)

60

Example 7-1 (*continued*)

QUESTIONS FOR DISCUSSION

1. How would you describe the texture of Ex. 7-1?

2. How would you define *chord, vertical sonority, individual harmony*?

3. What is a *triad*? a *seventh chord*?

4. What do we mean by *chord root, quality, position, inversion, voicing*?

5. How many different pitch classes are there in each of the chords in Ex. 7-1, measure 1? in measure 2? in measure 11? What is meant by *doubling* in chords? What is the relationship between doubling and dynamics in the example?

6. Most chords are made by "stacking up thirds." Where in Ex. 7-1 does Debussy create chords made of other intervals?

7. In spite of occasional chromaticism, Debussy's *Sarabande* has a strong tonic and an established mode (see mm. 20–22, 46–47, and 69–72). What is the tonic? What is the prevailing mode?

8. Look at the chord symbols in Ex. 1-2. What does the capital letter indicate? What does the expression "min" indicate? What is meant by the number 7? the number 9?

DEFINITIONS, PRINCIPLES, AND OBSERVATIONS

This chapter is devoted to the construction of chords (triads, seventh chords, and other sonorities). The way chords function in a harmonic context will be taken up in later chapters. Debussy's *Sarabande* from *Pour le Piano*, composed in 1901, is an excellent example of homophonic texture, consisting almost completely of melody supported by block chords.

A. DEFINITIONS

1. *Chord.* The sounding together of three or more tones. The tones may produce a consonant harmony or one with some degree of dissonance. The word *dischord* is often applied to chords of the highest degree of dissonance.

2. *Vertical sonority.* The sound produced by the tones present at any particular point in a piece of music. The sonority may be produced by a chord or by the interaction of tones in polyphony.

3. *Individual harmony.* One of a succession of related vertical sonorities.

4. *Tertian sonorities.* Chords or individual harmonies based on combinations of the interval of the third.

5. *Quartal sonorities.* Chords or individual harmonies based primarily on combinations of the interval of the perfect fourth, but also may involve intervals that can be derived from the pentatonic pitch collection: major second, perfect fifth, minor seventh, and to a lesser degree the major and minor third.

6. *Triad.* A chord consisting of three different pitch classes that are a third apart from one another in root position. The members are designated as root, third, and fifth.

7. *Seventh chord.* A chord consisting of four different pitch classes that are a third apart from one another in root position. The members are designated as root, third, fifth, and seventh.

8. *Chord root.* When a chord is arranged in a stack of thirds, the lowest note is the root. It serves as the fundamental pitch and is identified either by letter name or by roman numeral.

9. *Chord quality.* The harmonic character of a chord (in the case of triads) or its parts (in the case of seventh chords and other chord types).

10. *Chord position.* The arrangement of a chord depending on which of its members is the lowest note in the sonority. In root position, the lowest note is the root. In inversions, the lowest note is some note other than the root.

11. *Chord inversion.* A chord member other than the root is lowest in the sonority.

12. *Doubling.* Two or more notes in a chord are the same pitch class (the identical pitch or an equivalent octave). In the final measure of Ex. 7-1, the C♯ is doubled in six octaves, the E and the G♯ are doubled in two octaves each.

13. *Voicing.* The arrangement of a chord with regard to the distance between notes. In *close voicing*, notes are less than a fifth apart. In *open voicing*, notes may be a fifth or more apart, and the span of the chord will exceed an octave.

B. TYPES AND CONSTRUCTION OF CHORDS IN ROOT POSITION

1. Triads

Triad quality	Interval construction	Diagram	Examples in close voicing with C and F♯ as roots
Major	Root to third = M3 Third to fifth = m3 Root to fifth = P5	m3 M3	
Minor	Root to third = m3 Third to fifth = M3 Root to fifth = P5	M3 m3	
Diminished	Root to third = m3 Third to fifth = m3 Root to fifth = Dim 5	m3 m3	
Augmented	Root to third = M3 Third to fifth = m3 Root to fifth = Aug 5	M3 M3	

2. Seventh chords.

Quality of triad and seventh; symbol	Interval construction	Diagram	Examples in close voicing with C and F♯ as roots
Major-minor (Dominant Seventh Chord) Mm7	Root to third = M3 Third to fifth = m3 Fifth to Seventh = m3 Root to Seventh = m7	m3 m3 M3	
Minor-minor (Minor Seventh Chord) m7 or mm7	Root to third = m3 Third to fifth = M3 Fifth to Seventh = m3 Root to Seventh = m7	m3 M3 m3	
Major-major (Major Seventh Chord) M7 or MM7	Root to third = M3 Third to fifth = m3 Fifth to Seventh = M3 Root to Seventh = M7	M3 m3 M3	
Diminished-minor (Half-diminished Seventh Chord) ∅7 or dim-m7	Root to third = m3 Third to fifth = m3 Fifth to Seventh = M3 Root to Seventh = m7	M3 m3 m3	
Diminished-diminished (Full diminished Seventh Chord) °7 or dim-dim7	Root to third = m3 Third to fifth = m3 Fifth to Seventh = m3 Root to Seventh = dim 7	m3 m3 m3	
Minor-major mM7	Root to third = m3 Third to fifth = M3 Fifth to Seventh = M3 Root to Seventh = M7	M3 M3 m3	
Augmented-major Aug-M7	Root to third = M3 Third to fifth = M3 Fifth to Seventh = m3 Root to Seventh = M7	m3 M3 M3	

C. THE INVERSION OF CHORDS. Figures are used to indicate chord positions. They represent the interval distance from the lowest tone to each of the other members of the chord. The figures are presented from the top down in descending order, no matter how the chord has been voiced (see Ex. 7-2).

When indicating chords with roman numerals and in figured bass, the figures are abbreviated—not all are shown.

1. Major triads shown in root position, and in first and second inversion

	Root position	First inversion	Second inversion
Lowest note	Root	Third	Fifth
Intervals above bass	5 3	6 3	6 4
Figured bass symbol	Nothing	6	6 4
Examples of major chords with G and D♭ as roots			

2. Dominant seventh chords shown in root position, first, second, and third inversion

	Root position	First inversion	Second inversion	Third inversion
Lowest note	Root	Third	Fifth	Seventh
Intervals above bass	7 5 3	6 5 3	6 4 3	6 4 2
Figured bass symbol	7	6 5	4 3	4 2 or 2
Examples of Mm7 chords with D and F as roots				

3. Below are several chords of various types, positions, and voicings with an analysis showing root, chord type, and inversion symbol.

Example 7-2 Sample analysis of chords.

Root	F	D	G	Eb	F#	A	A	Eb	B	E
Type of chord	M	Mm7	m	M	MM	ø	mm	+	o	M
Inversion symbol	5 3	7	6 4	6 3	7	4 3	6 5	5 3	6 3	6 4

D. IDENTIFYING CHORDS IN A FIGURED BASS. A system was developed in the early Baroque era to indicate harmonies to be played by the continuo, usually a keyboard instrument (harpsichord or organ) or plucked string instrument (lute, theorbo, or guitar) to accompany a soloist or an ensemble. It consists of a bass part with figures that show not only harmonic tones but some nonharmonic tones as well. Below is a basic guide to the meaning of the symbols. A more complete guide appears in Appendix B.

The figures used with roman numerals are directly related to those used in figured bass notation.

1. All numbers and other symbols indicate interval distances to chord members or nonharmonic tones above the bass note. The actual chord voicing is left to the performer or the one who writes out a realization.

2. If no symbols appear at a point where a chord is expected, the chord is a diatonic triad with the bass tone as the root.

3. A sharp, flat, or natural by itself indicates the alteration of the third above the bass (in most cases also the third of the chord).

4. A slash across any number indicates that the chord member is to be raised by a half step.

5. Horizontal lines or dashes are sometimes used to indicate that the chord is to be sustained while the bass moves.

6. Two or more numbers appearing in succession above a single bass note, such as 4 3, 8 7, or 7 6, indicate melodic motion in one of the upper parts. This shows that a suspension, appoggiatura, or passing tone is expected against the bass tone.

7. Various abbreviations are common: 6 alone indicates $\frac{6}{3}$, 3 indicates $\frac{5}{3}$, 4 indicates a fifth and a fourth, with the fourth ready to resolve down. $\frac{6}{4}$ is not abbreviated.

8. An unusual stack of numbers such as $\frac{5}{2}$ is an indication that the note in the bass is a nonharmonic tone.

E. SUGGESTIONS FOR IDENTIFYING VERTICAL SONORITIES IN MUSICAL SCORES. Identifying chords given in the manner of Ex. 7-2 is relatively easy. Analyzing vertical sonorities encountered in musical scores is much more difficult. Below are some suggestions to help you with this task.

1. In your mind (or on scratch paper) assemble one of each pitch class present into a stack of thirds in close voicing. The lowest pitch in the stack is likely to be the root.

2. The root is the chord member most often doubled.

3. Note the quality of the lowest two thirds to determine the triad quality.

4. If there is a seventh above the root, note its quality. This plus the triad quality will determine the type of seventh chord.

5. If the lowest note in the chord you are examining is not the root, see if it is a member of the chord. If it is, determine the inversion. If it is not, it may be a pedal tone or nonharmonic tone.

F. INTERPRETATION OF CHORD SYMBOLS USED IN JAZZ AND POPULAR MUSIC. A *lead sheet* is a melody with chord symbols. These symbols, used in song books, jazz arrangements, and piano, guitar, and bass parts in stage band scores, have become relatively standard today; you may, however, encounter various alternate symbols, some of which are shown in the chart below.

1. The initial letter indicates the root of the chord.

2. If the initial letter appears alone or with an accidental, the chord is assumed to be a major triad. In some systems, a lowercase letter indicates a minor triad.

3. Letters or special symbols after the initial letter indicate chord quality.

4. Numbers indicate notes added to the basic triad. A 7 is assumed to be a minor seventh unless otherwise indicated. A 9 designates a diatonic ninth, unless an alteration symbol is given, and assumes the presence of a minor seventh as well.

5. Tall stacks such as eleventh and thirteenth chords usually assume a minor seventh and diatonic ninth unless otherwise indicated.

6. A letter following a slash indicates the bass note that is not the root.

7. Some systems use the minus sign (−) to indicate minor triads. This practice is not recommended because of the confusion that can occur with other uses of that symbol.

8. Below are some examples of commonly used lead sheet symbols.

Symbol	Alternate symbols	Description of the chord type	Chord members
G	GM, G Maj	Major triad	G-B-D
Dm	D Min, D −	Minor triad	D-F-A
B ° triad	B dim, B °	Diminished triad	B-D-F
C+	C Aug	Augmented triad	C-E-G♯
G7	GMm7	Dominant seventh	G-B-D-F
Em7	E min 7	Minor seventh chord	E-G-B-D
FM7	F Maj 7, F△7	Major seventh chord (or MM7)	F-A-C-E
B♭6	Gm7/B♭	Major triad with added sixth	B♭-D-F-G
C♯ °	C♯ ° 7, C♯dim-dm7	Diminished seventh chord	C♯-E-G-B♭
D sus 4		Triad with suspended fourth	D-G-A
C7/F	$\frac{C7}{F}$	Dominant seventh over a tonic pedal tone	F-C-E-G-B♭
F9	F7(9)	Dominant ninth chord	F-A-C-E♭-G
Bⵁ	B dim-m7, Bm7(♭5)	Half diminshed seventh chord	B-D-F-A
A7(♭9)		Minor ninth chord	A-C♯-E-G-B♭
C/G	C^6_4	Major triad, fifth in the bass	G-C-E

EXERCISES

EXERCISE 7-1 Identify each of these chords, showing root, chord type, and figures to show chord position.

Root   F   —— —— —— —— —— —— —— ——

Type of chord   M   —— —— —— —— —— —— —— ——

Inversion symbol $\frac{5}{3}$ —— —— —— —— —— —— —— ——

EXERCISE 7-2 Continue the identification of each of the vertical sonorities in this example.

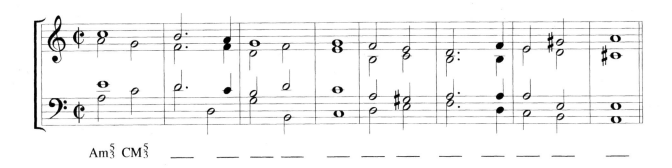

Am$^5_3$ CM$^5_3$ _____ _____ _____ _____ _____ _____ _____

EXERCISE 7-3 Continue the identification in lead sheet style of the chords in this excerpt from Ex. 7-1.

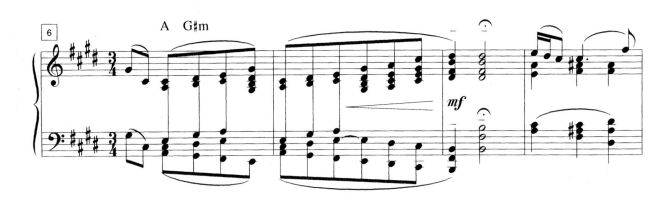

EXERCISE 7-4 Write block chords represented by these lead sheet symbols.

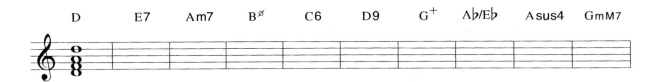

EXERCISE 7-5 Realize these figured bass examples by arranging the required pitches in the right hand. Use a variety of chord voicings and doublings. If the third of a chord is in the bass, omit it in the right hand.

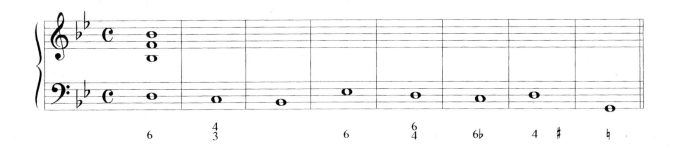

***EXERCISE 7-6** Copy out measures 46–55 of Ex. 7-1 and indicate as many vertical sonorities as you can using lead sheet symbols above the score. Label non-harmonic tones as well.

***EXERCISE 7-7** Write out the lowest part of Ex. 4-1, measures 49–69, and add figures in the style of a figured bass to show the harmonies.

***EXERCISE 7-8** Rescore this lead sheet example for voice and piano accompaniment. Doubling the melody in the piano part is optional.

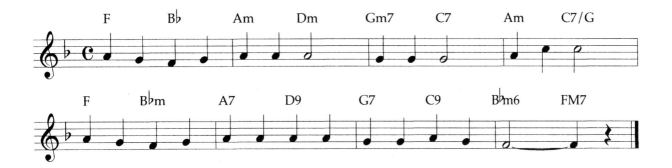

CHAPTER 8

MUSIC IN TWO PARTS

Example 8-1 "Metelitsa metet" ("Snow flurries"), Russian folk song, music by A. Varlamov.

Snow flurries blow down the street. I see my darling going through the storm.
Stay awhile, my dear one. Turn to me and let me gaze on your shining beauty.

Example 8-2 Two-Part Invention No. 7 by Johann Sebastian Bach (1685–1750).

Example 8-3 Duo from *Cartella musicale* by Adriano Banchieri (1568–1634).

QUESTIONS FOR DISCUSSION

1. Scan the intervals formed between the parts in the three examples above. What intervals are used most frequently? What intervals are used least frequently?

2. How does the pitch contour of the lower part compare to that of the upper part in each of the examples? How would you describe the rhythmic interplay between the parts in each example?

3. In Ex. 8-1, how do the notes in the bass relate to the chord symbols above the melody?

4. What is the prevailing rate of chord change in Ex. 8-1? If you were going to play chords on a guitar or a keyboard instrument to accompany Ex. 8-2, about how often would you expect to change chords?

5. Where are the phrase endings in the Russian folk song? Which of these are conclusive, and which are inconclusive?

6. Where are the strongest cadence points in Bach's E minor Invention? Some of the cadences establish a key other than the tonic. What are they?

7. In Ex. 8-3, the parts sometimes move in the same direction, sometimes in different directions, and sometimes one part is stationary while the other moves. How would you rank each of these types of motion in frequency of use?

8. There are a few places in Banchieri's Duo where the parts move in the same rhythm for a few notes. What intervals are used between the parts in those places? How are intervals used when there are two notes in one part against one in the other? more than two notes in one part against one in the other?

9. In $\frac{4}{2}$ meter, with the half note taken as the beat, the strong beats are on one and three. Something special happens when you find an interval of a second, seventh, or ninth on a strong beat in the Duo. Can you explain what it is?

10. How would you go about writing a bass part to go with a familiar melody?

11. How would you go about making a simple chordal accompaniment to a familiar melody?

DEFINITIONS, PRINCIPLES, AND OBSERVATIONS

The Russian folk song, Ex. 8-1, is a lead sheet with an accompanying bass part. The bass part supports the melody by giving it a harmonic foundation. The intervals between the bass tones and the melody most often are the ones found in tertian sonorities—triads and seventh chords. Most often the bass notes are chord roots, but occasionally they are other chord members, creating inversions. Decorative pitches appear in the bass part as well as the treble. The texture is relatively homophonic.

The bass part in Invention No. 7 by Bach also provides a harmonic foundation, especially at cadences, but at the same time, it develops the motives presented in the upper part through sequence and imitation. At the strong cadential points, the bass is given a falling fifth or rising fourth. This is typical of two-part Baroque polyphony.

The lower part in the Banchieri Duo is concerned almost exclusively with imitation of the upper part or initiating musical ideas that will be imitated by the upper part. At cadence points, the parts move to an octave or unison by step in contrary motion. The Duo is an example of late Renaissance counterpoint in two parts.

The three examples represent a span of about three hundred years, yet they share in the preferred use of thirds and sixths (and their equivalents, tenths and thirteenths). Perfect fifths, unisons, and octaves are next in rank. All three examples make far more use of stepwise motion than leaping motion. Most of the time, one of the parts moves while the other is stationary. There are, however, many places where the parts move in opposite direction. In the more rare occasions where they move in the same direction, they move in thirds or sixths (or their compound equivalents). Cadences conclude with unisons or octaves (or compound octaves).

A. DEFINITIONS

1. *Consonance and dissonance.* The meaning of these terms, as applied to intervals, has changed throughout history. The following definitions are more valid for Western music composed before the twentieth century:

Consonance. Intervals that are "pleasing," "harmonious," "pure," or "stable."

Dissonance. Intervals that are "unpleasant," "discordant," "impure," or "unstable."

It is more useful now to consider consonance and dissonance on a continuum where the intervals that sound more pure, stable, and lacking in tension are considered consonant, and the intervals that are more unstable, active, and higher in tension are considered dissonant.

For music composed roughly between 1500 and 1900, the *perfect consonances* are the perfect prime (unison), perfect fifth, and perfect octave. *Imperfect consonances* are major and minor thirds and major and minor sixths. Dissonances include all other intervals (seconds, sevenths, all augmented and diminished intervals including the tritone, and the perfect fourth).

For Western music composed since 1900 the perfect fourth, the major second (and major ninth), and the minor seventh have often been treated as imperfect consonances. In nontonal music, the words consonance and dissonance must be considered in terms of their historical and theoretical context.

2. *Conjunct and disjunct motion.* These terms were defined in Chapter 6 in regard to melody. In music written since about 1600, bass parts tend to have a somewhat larger amount of disjunct motion than the other parts. Music of all eras, however, is more conjunct than disjunct. Only in rare cases, mostly from our own century, can one find music where disjunct motion predominates.

3. *Relative motion of the parts.* The following types of relative motion are presented in order of most frequently used in two-part music:

Oblique motion. One part moves while the other is stationary.

Contrary motion. The parts move in the opposite direction from each other.

Parallel motion. The parts move in the same direction, retaining the interval size. Parallel motion is almost always in thirds or sixths.

Similar motion. The parts move in the same direction but the size of intervals changes.

Parallel unisons, octaves, and fifths have been almost universally avoided by composers except in doubling for emphasis or orchestral color. Parallel fifths became more common with the advent of chord planing in the early twentieth century. Parallel motion in any interval (except for unisons and octaves) has become more common in twentieth-century polyphony. (see Chapters 16 and 19 for more information on this subject.)

4. *Harmonic cadences.* In music for two parts, cadences tend to have harmonic attributes.

An *authentic cadence* describes a movement to tones of the tonic harmony (DO, MI or ME, SO) from tones of the dominant or dominant seventh harmony (SO, TI, RE, or FA)

A *plagal cadence* describes a movement to notes of the tonic from notes of the subdominant (FA, LA or LE, DO)

A *half* or *inconclusive cadence* describes a pause on a harmony that promises later completion (usually notes of the dominant)

A *deceptive cadence* describes a move toward the tonic (as in the authentic cadence) but resolves to a chord other than the tonic (usually the submediant harmony).

Modal cadences approach the tonic from a harmony that contains the most characteristic modal tones: RA-DO in the Phrygian, TE-DO in the Mixolydian, FI-SO in the Lydian, and so on.

Example 8-4 Two-voice cadences.

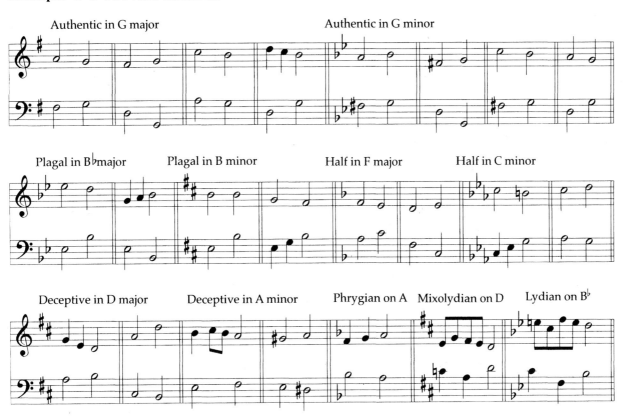

5. *Imitation.* Sharing of musical ideas among parts. The first seven notes in the right hand of Ex. 8-2 are imitated immediately in the left hand. This basic motive is treated in imitation throughout the piece. Imitation in Ex. 8-3 is of larger musical units. The first ten notes of the upper part are imitated in the lower part. A new idea beginning in the lower part at the end of measure 11 is treated to imitation (somewhat varied) in the upper part beginning in measure 14.

6. *Harmonic rhythm.* The rate of harmonic change. Harmonic rhythm is usually expressed in terms of the prevailing number of harmonies or chord changes per measure. In Ex. 8-1, the prevailing harmonic rhythm is one per measure, with occasional shifts to two per measure. In Ex. 8-2 there are one or two changes per measure, with a quickening of harmonic rhythm at the cadences. Since the Banchieri Duo was conceived as two melodies in counterpoint, the perception of changing harmonies is more subjective, and therefore the concept of harmonic rhythm is less relevant.

B. SUMMARY OF BASIC PRINCIPLES IN TWO-PART COUNTERPOINT. Although style changes after the Renaissance resulted in increased freedom in the use of dissonances, a stronger role of tonal harmony, and the use of instrumental figuration, the basic principles of two-part counterpoint have not changed significantly.

1. The parts maintain independence in their pitch and rhythmic motion. Pitch motion consists of a mixture of oblique, contrary, parallel, and similar motion. Rhythmic independence results from oblique motion but is occasionally relieved by parallel rhythm. In the example below, pitch motion is indicated between the staves. Rhythmic motion is indicated below the score.

Example 8-5 Independence of pitch and rhythmic motion in two-part counterpoint.

Pitch motion is indicated as follows: s = similar, o = oblique, c = contrary, p = parallel.

Rhythmic motion is indicated as follows: Par. = parallel rhythm, Ind. = independent rhythm.

2. Certain restrictions are observed by composers of two-part counterpoint with regard to the relative motion of the parts.

   a. Consonant intervals greatly outnumber dissonant intervals.
   b. Thirds and sixths are used far more frequently than any other intervals.
   c. Parallel intervals are generally restricted to imperfect consonances; parallel dissonances and parallel perfect consonances are avoided before the twentieth century.
   d. In similar motion the voices rarely leap to a perfect fifth or octave (referred to in counterpoint and harmony texts as *direct fifths* and *direct octaves*).

3. Some melodic principles in contrapuntal writing apply throughout the common practice period (roughly encompassing the Renaissance through the Romantic eras and much of tonal polyphony of the twentieth century).

   a. Conjunct motion predominates over disjunct motion.
   b. After a large leap (m6 or larger), the melody usually turns back in the opposite direction and proceeds by step.
   c. In Renaissance music, leaps larger than a perfect fourth were restricted to the perfect fifth, minor sixth, and octave. After about 1600, the use of other leaps came about with the development of more dissonant harmonies.
   d. Two voices rarely leap in similar motion, especially if one voice overlaps or crosses the other.
   e. Consecutive leaps tend to be perceived as belonging to a single harmony. For composers of the Renaissance, consecutive leaps were restricted to

triadic motion. Later, instrumental polyphony led to the increased use of arpeggios and broken-chord figures.

    f. The tritone is given special consideration. In Renaissance music, it is avoided as a melodic leap or outlined by changes in direction. These restrictions were abandoned with the use of chords involving the tritone.

4. *Species counterpoint.* A system for the study of counterpoint devised by Johann Fux in *Gradus ad Parnassum* (1725). Students are taught how to compose a counterpoint to a given *cantus firmus*, a short melody in whole notes. Some courses continue to use this method to this day. Below is a short summary of the principles of species counterpoint.

    a. *First Species* or *note-against-note counterpoint.* In Renaissance counterpoint, when the parts move note against note, the intervals between them are restricted to the consonances. After dominant seventh and diminished seventh chords became commonplace, the minor seventh and the tritone were occasionally admitted.

    b. *Second Species* or *two-against-one.* In Renaissance counterpoint, when a part has two notes against one in the other part, the first interval formed is consonant. The second of the two notes may create a consonance, or it may be a passing tone or a neighbor tone. With the advent of the appoggiatura and the accented passing tone, the first interval could be dissonant and the second consonant.

    c. *Third Species.* Three or more notes against one. In strict sixteenth-century counterpoint, third species denotes four notes to one, the first of which must be a consonance. The others may employ passing tones, neighbor tones, double neighbor groups, or the cambiata. A dissonance on the first tone became possible with the use of an appoggiatura or accented passing tone.

    d. *Fourth Species.* The use of suspensions and syncopations. The suspension figure has three elements, the *preparation,* the *suspension proper,* and the *resolution.* The table below shows requirements for each of these elements.

Element	Metric position	Harmonic interval	Other requirements
Preparation	Relatively strong	Consonant	Equal to or longer than the suspension proper
Suspension proper	Relatively strong	Dissonant	Equal to or shorter than the preparation
Resolution	Strong or weak depending on the length of the suspension	Consonant, but not a unison or octave	Step below the suspension; it should be a different pitch from the note used against the suspension.

The preparation and the suspension may appear as two notes tied together or as a single note that combines the duration of both preparation and suspension. In vocal music, the preparation and the suspension may have different words or syllables in the lyrics, and there is no tie.

The best suspension figures use the interval sequences 7-6, 4-3, and

2-3. Interval sequences 9-8, 2-1, and 7-8 are rare and should be avoided. Banchieri has used suspensions effectively, as shown in the example below.

Example 8-6 Suspensions in Ex. 8-3, measures 3–8.

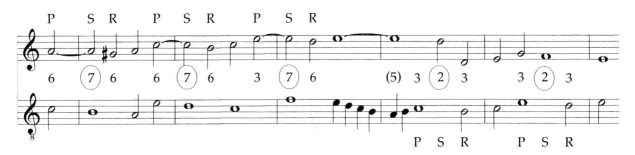

P = preparation, S = suspension proper, and R = resolution. Harmonic intervals are indicated between the staves. Those encircled are dissonances. The "(5)" indicates that the tied whole note E is not a suspension, but only a prolonged note that does not make a dissonance. When a note is sustained over a strong beat but does not make a dissonant interval, it is not treated like a suspension and may move up to the next note or leap in either direction.

Suspensions can be decorated by the insertion of one or more pitches before the resolution. By the end of the seventeenth century, the preparation could be a member of a dominant or diminished seventh chord, and a tone could be suspended that requires an upward resolution. This type of figure is called a *retardation*.

e. *Fifth Species.* "Florid" counterpoint involving the combined use of first through fourth species.

C. COMPOUND MELODY. A melody can give the impression of two parts through leaps between registers. Example 8-7 shows how the right hand of the Bach Minuet achieves this effect.

Example 8-7 Compound melody in Minuet I from Partita I in B flat by J. S. Bach (1685–1750), right-hand part.

D. ELABORATION OF A SIMPLE TWO-VOICE THEME. An effective way of creating variations is to add decorative pitches to a theme's basic pitches.

Example 8-8 Old English tune "The Carman's Whistle" with variation by elaboration.

E. CHOOSING CHORDS FOR A LEAD SHEET

1. Play or sing through the melody and mark the places where you feel chord changes are needed. Jazz musicians refer to the sequence of chords in a lead sheet as "the changes."

2. Try playing various chords at these places. The note in the melody where you want a chord is likely to be a member of that chord. For example, if you were to supply chord symbols for "Twinkle, twinkle, little star," written in C Major, the first note will be C. It could be the root of a C chord, the third of Am, or the fifth of F. It could even be the seventh of D7. A quick trial of these chords would soon result in the choice of a C chord. You probably want a chord change for "little," which will be on A. The A could be the root of an A chord (major or minor), the third of an F chord, or the fifth of a Dm (or major) chord. Your likely choice will be the F chord.

Note in Example 8-9 that the C chord can be sustained through measure 1, but the suggested change to C first inversion (C with E in the bass) improves the flow of the harmonic rhythm, which is two changes per bar. Some different chords have been used in the repeated part of the second phrase for the sake of variety.

3. The notes of the melody where chord changes occur will be various chord members. Moving the chords along in parallel with the melody creates a poor effect.

Example 8-9 Lead sheet for the beginning of "Twinkle, twinkle, little star."

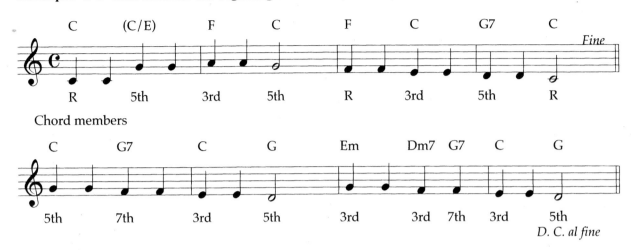

Chord members

4. Most melodies will suggest a relatively even rate of harmonic changes—a stable harmonic rhythm. If one chord continues for two measures, it would not be appropriate for the next measure to have four chord changes. It is common, however, for the harmonic rhythm to increase at cadence points.

5. In some cases two or three different chords will seem appropriate for a particular note in the melody, and sometimes a particular choice of chord will lead you to make a particular choice for the next chord. Keep in mind, however, that your choice of chords should be suitable to the melodic style. A set of changes involving seventh, ninth, and thirteenth chords would not be appropriate for a simple hymn tune like "O come, all ye faithful."

F. REDUCTION TO A TWO-VOICE FRAMEWORK. In the example below, the basic pitches of the violin part are shown above the score, and the basic pitches of the continuo part are shown below the score.

Example 8-10 Aria 5 from *Die Kleine Kammermusik,* Partita I by Georg Philipp Telemann (1681–1767).

Example 8-10 (*continued*)

The harmonic rhythm in the example is two to four per measure. It is a period whose first phrase ends with an inconclusive (half) cadence in measure 3, and whose second phrase ends with a conclusive (authentic) cadence in measure 7. Both phrases begin with the same musical idea.

EXERCISES   **EXERCISE 8-1** Enter chord symbols in the boxes that would be appropriate for this familiar tune.

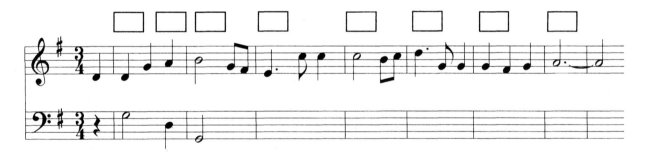

EXERCISE 8-2 Using the chords you chose in Ex. 8-1 as a guide, continue the bass line. You may use the third of the chord occasionally and a few passing tones or neighbor tones.

EXERCISE 8-3 Complete this canon at the octave below. Indicate by size the intervals formed between the parts (use 2 for ninths, 3 for tenths, and so on), circle those that are considered dissonant for this style (2, 4, 7, ⁺4, º5) and identify them with p = passing tone, n = neighbor tone, and S = suspension.

EXERCISE 8-4 Complete the bass using mostly quarter notes and half notes.

EXERCISE 8-5 Continue this little two-voice Baroque dance strain using the given framework.

*EXERCISE 8-6** Write two variations on the Elizabethan tune, "John come kisse me now," by elaboration of the simple version given below. Use some eighth-note figures in the first and some sixteenth-note figures in the second.

*EXERCISE 8-7 Write a two-voice passacaglia with three or four variations on this bass. In the final variation, you may add some decorative tones in the bass.

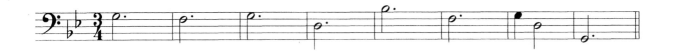

CHAPTER 9

MUSIC IN THREE OR MORE PARTS

The examples below show music in three, four, and five parts respectively. Perform them in class and compare them before considering the questions that follow them.

Example 9-1 "The Ash Grove," English folk song.

Example 9-2 Chorale: "Aus meines Herzens Grunde," harmonized by J. S. Bach (1685–1750).

*) The alto in bar 17 has been simplified from the original.

Example 9-3 Chanson: "Françion vint l'autre jour" by Pierre Bonnet (fl. 1600)

Françion came the other day and found me all alone. He spoke to me then of love in such a discreet manner that I will never give my love to anyone but Françion.

QUESTIONS FOR DISCUSSION

1. If you were to convert Ex. 9-1 to a lead sheet, what would the chord symbols be from the beginning up to the repeat bar? What is the prevailing harmonic rhythm?

2. If you were to convert Ex. 9-1 to a figured bass, what figures would be needed with the bass from the beginning to the repeat bar?

3. How can you use the information obtained by answering the first two questions to produce a roman numeral chord analysis?

4. What kinds of harmonic and nonharmonic decorative pitches do you find in the first phrase of Ex. 9-1 (up to the repeat bar)?

5. Where are the cadences located in the three examples? What kinds of cadences are they?

6. Consider the harmonic rhythm in Ex. 9-2 and in Ex. 9-3. How do the three examples differ in their use of harmonic rhythm?

7. Scan all three examples for pitch movement of the parts (voice leading). How often do you find all parts moving from one harmony to the next in parallel or similar motion?

8. How many instances can you find where the fifth of a chord is in the bass? Where a triad built on the leading tone is used in root position?

9. What chord members are most often doubled in each of the examples? What chord members are least often doubled in the examples? Are there any scale degrees that are almost never doubled?

10. How can you have a seventh chord with only three parts? Are there any seventh chords in Ex. 9-1?

11. What is the largest interval Bach has allowed between the soprano and alto parts? Between the alto and tenor parts? Between the tenor and bass parts? How does this compare to the interval spacing between consecutive parts in the chanson and the folk song?

12. When the bass part goes very low, how far above do you find the tenor part? Why is it appropriate to allow more than an octave between bass and tenor?

DEFINITIONS, PRINCIPLES, AND OBSERVATIONS

In Chapter 7 we examined chord construction. Now we will put these chords in the context of functional harmony and discuss how harmonic progression is achieved in music of three or more parts. When the information provided by a lead sheet is combined with that provided by a figured bass, the result leads to roman numeral chord analysis, an important tool for indicating harmonic function.

A. THE ROMAN NUMERAL SYSTEM

1. The chord root is indicated by a roman numeral that corresponds to the scale degree upon which the chord is built. For example, a D Major triad in the key of A Major is the IV chord.

2. The case of the roman numeral, with or without other symbols, indicates the chord's triadic quality. Upper case indicates major triad quality. Lower case indicates minor triad quality. If a $^+$ is added, an augmented triad quality is indicated. If a $^\circ$ is added, a diminished triad quality is indicated.

QUALITY OF DIATONIC TRIADS

Root Scale Degree	Scale Degree Name	Triad Quality in Major Keys	Symbol	Triad Quality in Minor Keys	Symbol	Modal Alternates in Minor Keys
$\hat{1}$	Tonic	Major	I	Minor	i	I♯ (Picardy Third)
$\hat{2}$	Supertonic	Minor	ii	Diminished	ii°	ii
$\hat{3}$	Mediant	Minor	iii	Major	III	III+
$\hat{4}$	Subdominant	Major	IV	Minor	iv	IV
$\hat{5}$	Dominant	Major	V	Major	V	v
$\hat{6}$	Submediant	Minor	vi	Major	VI	
$\hat{7}$	Leading tone	Diminished	vii°	Diminished	vii°	VII (V of III)

3. If no figures appear next to the roman numeral, root position is indicated. The figures $\frac{5}{3}$ may be used to show when a chord has moved from an inversion to root position.

4. Figures indicate the presence of sevenths (and ninth, eleventh, or thirteenth chords in root position) and inversions of triads and seventh chords. They always represent interval distance measured above the bass (see Chapter 7, C-1 and 2).

5. Accidentals indicate alterations to diatonic chords. The symbol I♯ indicates raised third in a tonic chord that is normally minor, the "Picardy third."

6. The diminished and augmented signs (+ and °) next to a number indicate specific chords. The symbol +6 indicates an augmented sixth chord, the symbol °7 indicates a (full) diminished seventh chord, and the symbol ø7 indicates a half-diminished seventh chord.

7. A sharp or flat in front of a roman numeral shows alteration of the root up or down a half step. For example, ♭VII indicates a lowered leading tone chord. In the key of D minor, ♭VII is a C major triad.

Example 9-4 The opening measures of Ex. 9-1 with roman numeral chord analysis. Nonharmonic tones are circled.

Ab: V   I₆ $\frac{5}{3}$ V₆   I   6   vi   ii₆ $\frac{5}{3}$ 6   V   6 $\frac{5}{3}$ I₆

B. PRIMARY, SECONDARY, AND MODAL CHORDS

1. The *primary chords* are those built on the tonic, dominant, and subdominant in major and minor keys. These chords most clearly define the tonality, and they are employed in conclusive cadences and strong progressions.

2. The *secondary chords* are those built on the supertonic, mediant, and submediant in major and minor keys. These chords provide variety and smoothness in harmonic progression.

3. The *leading tone chords* most often have a dominant function. The vii° triad is very rarely encountered in root position in music for four or more parts because of the tritone between the root in the bass and the fifth of the chord. It is occasionally used in three-part music in the configuration shown in Ex. 9-5 b. When a seventh is added to the leading-tone triad, it may be used in root position, regardless of the number of parts.

Example 9-5 Some common voicings of the leading-tone chord. Circled notes are passing tones.

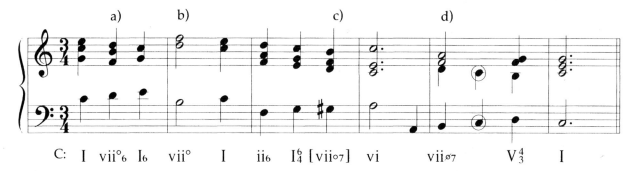

a) in first inversion, four parts.
b) in root position, three parts.
c) diminished seventh chord, root position, dominant function to the A minor chord that follows it. The brackets indicate a secondary dominant function, discussed at length in Chapter 10.
d) half diminished seventh chord, root position.

4. The *modal alternative chords* shown in the chart above result from the raising or lowering of degrees $\hat{6}$ and $\hat{7}$ in the melodic form of the minor. When degree $\hat{6}$ is raised, the supertonic chord quality becomes minor and the subdominant chord becomes major. With raised $\hat{7}$ the mediant chord becomes augmented. With lowered $\hat{7}$ the dominant chord becomes minor.

C. ROOT MOVEMENT

1. Strong harmonic progression results from root movement by perfect fourth or perfect fifth up or down. Some examples are I–IV, iii–vi, iv–i, VI–III, V–ii, V–I. The strongest and most common root movement in music of the Baroque, Classical, and Romantic eras is by falling fifth or rising fourth. One of the most common progressions is a sequence based on the Circle of Fifths. In Ex. 9-1 beginning with beat 3 of measure 2, the harmonies are vi–ii–V–I–IV leading to the final cadence. Root motion by falling fourth or rising fifth, however, is common in the Renaissance, in modal folk music, and in the blues progression.

2. Weaker harmonic progression results from root movement by third. This is due to the fact that diatonic chords whose roots are a third apart have two common tones, with only one tone changing in the progression. Some examples are I–iii, I–vi, IV–ii, VI–i, IV–vi.

3. Smooth progression results from root movement by step. Stepwise progression creates a strong feeling of forward motion. Some examples are IV–V, V–vi, iii–ii, vi–V.

D. CADENCES. The simple chorale below demonstrates the use of five common cadence types in a four-part homophonic setting.

Example 9-6 Common cadence types.

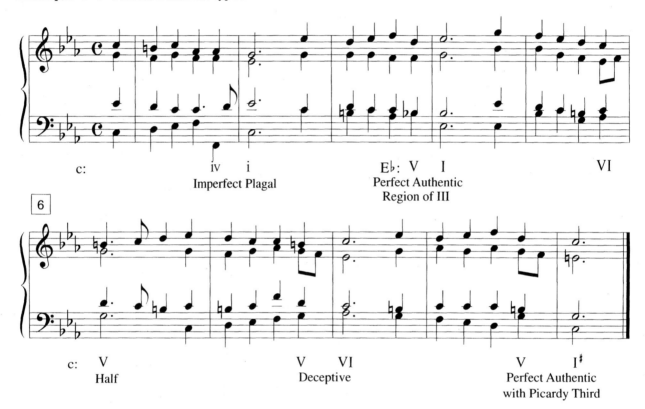

1. The strongest and most common cadence in tonal music is the *authentic cadence.* In its simplest form it is V–I in major and V–i in minor. The dominant chord may include a seventh. Since the vii° or the vii°7 can have a dominant function, they can be used in an authentic cadence instead of the dominant itself. Remember, however, that the vii° should be used in first inversion, especially in music of four or more parts. In Ex. 9-1, authentic cadences appear in measures 8 (vii°6–I) and 16 (in E♭ major: V–I). In Ex. 9-2, authentic cadences appear in measures 7 (V–I), 14 (in C major: V7–I), and 21 (V–I).

2. The *plagal cadence* is more common in the Renaissance than in later periods. Its simplest form is IV–I in major and iv–i in minor. In Ex. 9-3, a plagal cadence appears in measure 11 (IV–I).

3. The *half cadence* is an inconclusive cadence. It is a pause on the dominant, promising later fulfillment in a conclusive cadence, usually at the end of the next phrase. In Ex. 9-2, half cadences appear in measures 4, 10, and 18 (I–V in all cases).

4. A *deceptive cadence* is one in which some other chord is substituted for the expected tonic resolution. Its most common form is V–vi in major and V–VI in minor. Other possibilities are V–iii (or III), V–♭VI, and V to a neighboring °7 chord (in C major: G–B–D to F♯–A–C–E♭).

5. A *perfect* cadence is one that resolves with the tonic in both the highest and lowest voices. The letters PAC indicate a perfect authentic cadence.

6. An *imperfect* cadence is one that resolves with some other tone than the tonic in either the highest or lowest voices or both. IAC indicates an imperfect authentic cadence. In Ex. 9-3, measure 2, the cadence is imperfect, since the highest voice has the third of the chord. The cadence in measure 5 is a PAC.

7. A *regional* cadence is a conclusive cadence in a key other than the tonic, most commonly the key of the dominant or the relative minor or major, but regional cadences to other closely related keys are possible as well. Regional cadences are usually prepared by secondary dominant chords, discussed in detail in Chapter 10. In Ex. 9-1 the cadence in measure 16 is a perfect authentic cadence in the region of the dominant. In Ex. 9-2 the cadence in measure 14 is an imperfect authentic cadence in the region of the subdominant. The Bach chorales are rich in the use of regional cadences.

E. PRINCIPLES OF PART WRITING. These principles apply to music of the "common practice period," roughly from 1600 to 1900, including music of the twentieth century that adheres to traditional tonal part-writing practices. They are generalities, not hard-and-fast rules.

1. Voice leading

a. Movement from one chord to another is accomplished generally by stepwise motion, except in the bass part, where leaps may be used as well.

b. Tones common to adjacent harmonies are often retained in the same voice.

c. Active tones are resolved by step: RE-DO, FA-MI (ME), LA (LE)-SO, TI-DO.

d. The leading-tone and tones that have been raised by an accidental resolve up. Chord sevenths and tones that have been lowered by accidental resolve down. Degrees $\hat{6}$ and $\hat{7}$ of the Melodic Minor are affected by this principle. In general, when the melodic goal is the tonic, LA and TI are used. When the goal is the dominant note, TE and LE are used.

e. Thirds, sixths, and tenths are overwhelmingly preferred for voices in parallel motion. Parallel fourths may be used between upper voices. All other intervals, especially fifths and octaves, are discouraged for parallel motion.

f. Parallel and similar motion of all parts is avoided except for parallel first inversion chords (fauxbourdon) or motion within a single harmony.

g. Outer parts move in contrary or oblique motion more often than similar or parallel motion.

h. The members of a tritone resolve in opposite direction by step. The $^+4$ resolves outward; the $°5$ resolves inward.

i. Most dissonances should be approached and left by step. Exceptions are the appoggiatura, which can be approached by leap, the escape tone, which is left by a leap, and the double neighbor tone, which contains the leap of a third.

j. Leaps of augmented or diminished intervals are generally avoided unless both tones belong to the harmony.

2. Doubling

a. *With any number of parts*: Doubling the leading-tone is avoided, as well as chord sevenths, ninths, elevenths, or thirteenths, and most altered tones.

b. *In three parts*: When all members of a triad are present, there will be no doubling. When seventh chords are used, the fifth is usually omitted. The root is most often doubled. It may even be used in all parts in very close voicing or at strong cadences. The third may be doubled in minor triads and in major triads if it is approached by step in contrary motion. The fifth is not doubled since the root or the third would then be omitted.

Example 9-7 Doubling in the opening measures of Ex. 9-1.

b. *In four parts*: The root is doubled most often in triads. The fifth may occasionally be doubled. The third may be doubled in minor triads and in major triads when approached in contrary motion by step. Seventh chords usually appear with all members, but the fifth may be omitted when the root is doubled. In the deceptive progression V–vi (or VI in minor), the third is doubled in the submediant chord. The third is doubled in the vii°6 chord.

Example 9-8 Doubling in the opening measures of Ex. 9-2.

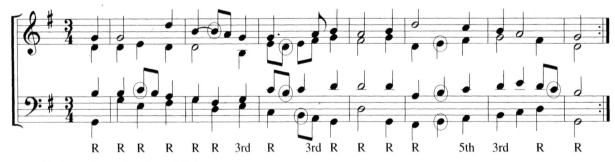

Nonharmonic tones have been circled.

d. *In five or more parts*: Any chord member may be doubled, but the root is most often doubled or trebled. There is usually more disjunct motion in order to avoid parallel fifths and octaves.

Example 9-9 Doubling in the opening measures of Ex. 9-3.

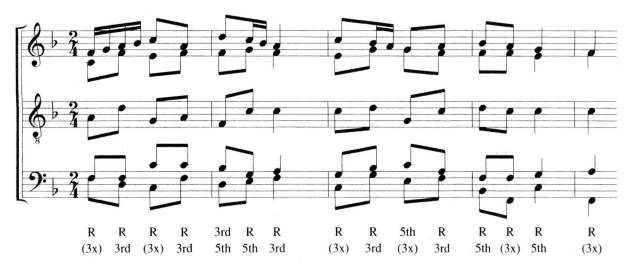

R	R	R	R	3rd	R	R		R	R	5th	R		R	R	R		R
(3x)	3rd	(3x)	3rd	5th	5th	3rd		(3x)	3rd	(3x)	3rd		5th	(3x)	5th		(3x)

3. Voicing

   a. In three-part music, voicing may be very close (as in the first two measures of Ex. 9-1) or open (as in Ex. 9-1, measure 3). The middle part may
   be independent of the outer parts, or it may move in conjunction with one
   of the outer parts. The interval distance from the middle part to either of
   the other parts may exceed an octave.

   b. In music for four parts, the distance between soprano and alto and between alto and tenor rarely exceeds an octave. The distance between bass
   and tenor, however, often exceeds an octave. Ex. 9-2 bears this out.

   c. Close voicing in low register tends to sound muddy. When the bass descends to first-line G or lower, the tenor is usually a fifth or more above it.

4. Inversions

   a. The figures below demonstrate the stability of a triad in root position, first
   inversion, and second inversion. Root position is solidly stable, first inversion is less stable, and second inversion is unstable.

   The stability of root position harmonies is such that they can be used for
   the beginning and ending of a progression. First inversion harmonies provide variety and help in the feeling of motion in a progression. Because
   of its unstability, the second inversion is restricted in its use.

   b. The cadential $^6_4$ prepares the authentic cadence. In the common cadential
   progression I$^6_4$–V–I, the sixth and fourth above the bass act like double
   appoggiaturas to the fifth and third of the dominant chord. For this reason, some analytical systems prefer to use the symbols V$^{6-5}_{4-3}$.

c. A triad in $^6_4$ position can be the result of passing or neighbor motion. It can also result from a double appoggiatura or arpeggio like motion in the bass.

Example 9-10 Typical uses of the second inversion triad.

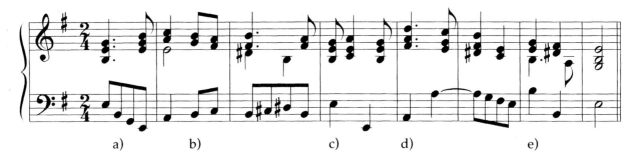

a) arpeggio $^6_4$.

b) Passing $^6_4$.

c) Neighbor $^6_4$.

d) Appoggiatura $^6_4$.

e) Cadential $^6_4$.

d. Second inversion triads are usually approached in the bass by step. The arpeggio $^6_4$, the appoggiatura $^6_4$, and the cadential $^6_4$ chords, however, can be approached in the bass by step or by leap.

| **EXERCISES** | **EXERCISE 9-1** Complete the chart below showing the types of diatonic seventh chords for each degree of the major and minor scale. The syllables in parentheses show which form of the sixth and seventh scale degrees in minor are used in the chords. |

Scale Degree Name	Symbol in Major	Triad and 7th Quality	Symbol in Minor	Triad and 7th Quality	Modal Alternates in Minor Keys	Triad and 7th Quality
Tonic	I^7	Major-major	i^7	Minor-minor	$i\sharp^7$ (TI)	Minor-major
Supertonic	ii^7					
Mediant	iii^7					
Subdominant	IV^7					
Dominant	V^7	Major-minor	V^7	Major-minor	v^7 (TE)	
Submediant	vi^7					
Leading-tone	$vii^{\emptyset 7}$					

EXERCISE 9-2 Make a three-part arrangement for piano of the Russian folk song, Ex. 8-1 by adding a middle part.

EXERCISE 9-3 Make a copy of "The Ash Grove," Ex. 9-1, then give a roman numeral analysis, using Ex 9-4 as a guide. Circle the nonharmonic tones.

EXERCISE 9-4 Provide an alto and tenor part for the chorale melody, "O Welt, ich muss dich lassen," which has been given a figured bass based on a harmonization by J. S. Bach.

EXERCISE 9-5 Make a roman numeral chord analysis of the four-part harmonization you completed in Exercise 9-4.

EXERCISE 9-6 Write five connected variations (a passacaglia) on this figured bass as follows: Var. 1: Cello alone. Var. 2: Violin 1 and Cello. Var. 3: Violin 1, Violin 2, and Cello. Var. 4: Violin 1, Violin 2, Viola, and Cello. Var. 5: Violin 1, Violin 2, Violin 3, Viola, Cello.

*****EXERCISE 9-7** Suppose you wish to have your middle school choir perform "Françion," Ex. 9-3, but the choir can manage only three parts, Soprano, Alto, and Baritone. The baritones have a lower limit of first-space A. Make an arrangement of the little chanson that would be within your choir's capabilities.

*EXERCISE 9-8 Now suppose you wish to perform "The Ash Grove" with your high school choir that is used to singing four-part SATB choral music. Look up the lyrics in an English folk song book, and make an arrangement for SATB using Ex. 9-1 as a point of departure.

*EXERCISE 9-9 Make a five-part choral setting of one of the following:

   a. "Were you there" (Negro spiritual)

   b. "Amazing Grace" (American hymn)

   c. "Drink to me only with thine eyes" (folk song)

   d. "Shalom Chaverim" (Hebrew melody)

CHAPTER 10

ALTERED CHORDS I
Secondary Dominants

Example 10-1 Theme and Var. 3 from *Variations on a Theme by Haydn*, Op. 56b by Johannes Brahms (1833–1897).

Example 10-1 (*continued*)

Example 10-1 (*continued*)

Example 10-1 (*continued*)

Example 10-1 (*continued*)

Example 10-1 (*continued*)

QUESTIONS FOR DISCUSSION

1. Brahms has made a setting of the theme that preserves Haydn's largely diatonic harmonies. There are, however, a few chords with altered tones. What is the function of these alterations?

2. The chords that have altered tones are of what types?

3. Compare Variation 3 with the theme. What has been retained and what has been changed?

4. In Variation 3 there are many more altered chords than in the theme. What can you say about their harmonic function?

5. Name some well-known folk songs or popular songs that use harmonies that function like those we have examined in Ex. 10-1.

DEFINITIONS, PRINCIPLES, AND OBSERVATIONS

A. SECONDARY DOMINANT CHORDS

1. Chords that function as dominant to chords other than the tonic are called *secondary dominant chords* or *applied dominant chords*. For example, in the key of C:

   A D Major chord functions like a dominant to a G Major chord. It is indicated as V of V.

   An A7 functions like a dominant seventh of a D minor chord. It is indicated as V7 of ii.

   A G♯ diminished chord, first inversion, functions like a leading-tone chord to an A minor chord. It is indicated as vii°⁶ of vi.

   An E full diminished seventh chord functions like a leading-tone diminished seventh chord to an F Major chord. It is indicated as vii°⁷ of IV.

2. Secondary dominant chords may take the form of triads, major-minor seventh chords, or full diminished seventh chords. They may appear in root position or in any inversion.

3. Secondary dominant chords are usually conspicuous because of altered tones. A raised tone indicates a leading tone to the root of the chord of resolution. A lowered tone indicates a tone that functions like FA in the key of the chord of resolution.

4. In Roman numeral nomenclature, secondary dominants may be indicated in several ways as shown:

With "of"	With a slash	With a bracket
V⁷ of vi vi	V⁷ / vi vi	[V⁷] vi

For the purposes of this text, the indication with the bracket will be used.

Example 10-2 Secondary dominant chords in C Major.

In Variation 3 of Ex. 10-1, Brahms uses several diminished seventh chords as decorative secondary dominants. Example 10-3 is a harmonic reduction of mm. 1–10 of the variation showing chord analysis. Note that m. 7 is a sequence of m. 6 up a fourth, creating a movement to the region of the subdominant. The regional progression is indicated by a horizontal line with a IV underneath.

Example 10-3 Secondary dominants in measures 1–10 of Var. 3 from Ex. 10-1.

*This is an incomplete diminished chord that has a dominant function to the following chord.

EXERCISES   EXERCISE 10-1 Supply missing notes in the lower three parts.

D: I [V⁷] vi   ii⁶ [V⁶₅] V ——— I⁶ [V⁴₃] IV [V⁴₃] ii V⁷ I

EXERCISE **10-2** Complete this harmonic reduction and chord analysis of the chorale theme from Ex. 10-1.

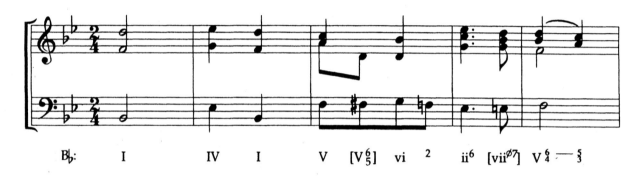

B♭:   I   IV   I   V [V⁶₅] vi   2   ii⁶ [vii°⁷] V⁶₄ — ⁵₃

EXERCISE **10-3** Supply parts for Violin II and Viola for this string quartet passage, then show a chord analysis below the cello part.

*EXERCISE **10-4** Using Example 10-3 as a model, make a harmonic reduction and chord analysis of Variation 3 from Example 10-1.

*EXERCISE 10-5 Provide a realization (right-hand part) for the continuo of this short piece for violin and continuo. Write a roman numeral chord analysis.

Part Two

CHAPTER 11

TEXTURE AND VARIATION

Example 11-1 Excerpts from *32 Variations on an Original Theme* by Ludwig van Beethoven (1770–1827).

Example 11-1 (*continued*)

Example 11-1 (*continued*)

QUESTIONS FOR DISCUSSION

1. What is your definition of the word "texture" when applied to objects such as cloth, bread, soil, paintings?

2. What is "texture" when applied to music?

3. What does "variation" have to do with "texture?"

4. How would you describe changes in texture as you compare the variations by Beethoven given in Ex. 11-1?

5. What has Beethoven retained in all of the variations?

6. If you were writing a set of variations, what things would you consider changing, and what things would you retain?

7. What is the difference between a passacaglia and a theme and variations?

DEFINITIONS, PRINCIPLES, AND OBSERVATIONS

The word "texture" is used to describe the character or quality produced by the interweaving or interaction of the materials from which an object is made. We use ordinary words such as "heavy," "thin," "smooth," and "rough," to characterize the texture of cloth, soil, painted surfaces, and the like. We sometimes apply these words to musical texture, but we also use more specific terms such as *homophonic, polyphonic, layered, patterned.* The texture of a passage of music results from the interaction of the materials used—the deployment of its parts, or the interplay of the musical dimensions discussed in Chapter 1.

A. TERMS USED TO DESCRIBE MUSICAL TEXTURES

1. *Monophony.* A single line of music. Examples of monophony are chant, unaccompanied song, or music for solo instrument. The melody can be doubled in the same or different registers or with voices and instruments. Much of the music of non-Western cultures is monophonic.

2. *Homophony.* Melody and subordinate accompanying parts. The melody is often the uppermost part (hymns, songs), but it may also appear as the lowest part (as in Schumann's "Happy Farmer"), a middle part (as in Rubenstein's "Melody in F"), or doubled in the outside parts with harmony between (as in "Un bel di" from *Madama Butterfly* by Puccini). In Ex. 11-1, the theme, Var. XII, and Var. XXX are clearly homophonic in texture.

3. *Polyphony.* Music for two or more parts or voices, each of which maintains its musical identity. Since this definition can be applied also to the word *counterpoint,* polyphony can be defined as "music in a contrapuntal texture." Although not required, polyphonic music is often imitative—that is, the parts share musical ideas. Rounds and canons are special cases of polyphony, since the imitation is fixed and continuous. In most polyphonic music the parts are of equal importance, but in some genres one part has a special role, such as the chorale melody in a chorale prelude or the *cantus firmus* in a Renaissance mass. Example 11-1 Var. XXII is imitative and therefore polyphonic.

4. *Heterophony.* The simultaneous performance of two or more different versions of a single melody. It often consists of a sung melody accompanied by an instrument (or instruments) playing an ornamented version of the melody. Musics outside of the Western tradition often employ heterophonic texture.

5. *Simultaneity.* When used as a word defining texture, it refers to two or more strands of unrelated music sounding together. This texture was exploited by Charles Ives in several pieces (*The Unanswered Question,* Symphony No. 4).

6. *Hybrid textures.* Music that combines elements of homophony and polyphony. In Ex. 11-1 Var. XVII, the texture is hybrid since it is imitative in the upper parts, accompanied by a subordinate broken-chordal pattern.

7. *Layered textures.* Music in layers distinguished by rhythm, pattern, instrumentation, or other distinctive musical element. Ex. 1-1, the opening of Schumann's *Kinderszenen,* three distinct layers can be observed: the melody on top, a broken-chord pattern in the middle, and a rhythmically regular bass line on the bottom.

8. *Patterned textures.* Music making extensive use of repeating patterns. Variations from the Classical period often use patterns as their chief point of departure from the theme. Once the pattern is presented, it adjusts to the changing harmonies as the variation progresses. Minimalist music, also called *pattern music,* such as that by Steve Reich and John Adams, is easily recognized by the continuous repetition and development of patterns.

B. OTHER FACTORS THAT AFFECT TEXTURE

1. *Number and deployment of parts.* A duet has a thin texture compared to an eight-voice motet. The close spacing of voices in a barbershop quartet produces a different texture from the widely spaced voices in some wood wind quintet music. Textural variety can be achieved in ensemble music by changing the number and spacing of parts sounding together at different parts of a piece. The stunning effect of polychoral music is due largely to the changing textures provided by the deployment of the different choruses as well as their spatial separation. Music for keyboard allows for quick changes from a single tone to many. The theme in Ex. 11-1 begins with three tones struck together, then increases to eight in measure 6, ending in measure 8 with single tones. Var. VIII maintains a two-part contrapuntal texture throughout.

2. *Diatonic versus chromatic textures.* The texture is affected by the amount of chromaticism used. Since the theme in Ex. 11-1 makes use of a chromatic harmonic progression, all of the variations will have a chromatic texture. In contrast, Ex. 4-1 is purely diatonic. The chromaticism of Beethoven's *32 Variations* is harmonic, for the most part. Chromaticism can be decorative, as in the variation in Ex. 6-6.

3. *Articulation.* The smooth texture of Var. XVII, which is legato, contrasts markedly with the brittle texture of Var. XXII, which is staccato.

4. *Tessitura.* Beethoven creates a lighter texture in Var. XIII by limiting the music to middle and high tessituras. A darker texture is evident in Var. XII, which is limited to a lower tessitura.

5. *Broken versus continuous textures.* Beethoven's theme consists of several gestures, heard as succession of subphrases, each two measures long. A much more continuous texture appears in Var. XXX, which has no breaks at all. Minimalist music tends to be continuous in texture, whereas pointillistic music is broken in texture.

6. *Rhythmic density.* The speed of rhythmic activity. A patter song from a Gilbert and Sullivan opera has a much higher rhythmic density than a love song.

7. *Harmonic rhythm.* The rate of harmonic change in a piece of music. The term is briefly discussed in Chapter 8. Bach's chorales usually have a harmonic rhythm of one per quarter note. In the "Alla Turca" movement of Mozart's Sonata in A, K. 331, the first harmony continues for four measures, the next for more than two measures. In some pieces the harmonic rhythm is unstable or unpredictable. Examples can be found in highly dramatic music, such as opera recitative.

C. VARIATION TYPES AND TECHNIQUES

1. *Continuous variations.* The chaconne, the passacaglia, and the ground are considered continuous variations because there are no breaks between variations. Often they are linked so that the last measure of one variation makes a cadence in the first measure of the next. The point of departure for these types of variation is a succession of bass tones that repeats in each variation with new music added above. Sometimes the point of departure is a succession of harmonies. When musicians play "the blues," they are making variations over a given set of harmonies. When a jazz soloist "takes choruses," the formal procedure is the same as in continuous variations, with "the changes" (the chord progression of the tune) remaining constant.

2. *Theme and variations.* The melody, harmony, and form of the theme provide the point of departure for each variation, and there is usually a break between variations. What changes most dramatically in each variation is the

texture. In Beethoven's variations, Ex. 11-1, the texture of each variation is unique.

3. *Character variations.* Each variation, while musically based on the theme, takes its character from a genre (waltz, toccata, and so on) or an extramusical idea. Variations of this type describe places, people, events, or are set in the styles of various composers. For example, in Bach's *Goldberg Variations*, some genres represented are *fughetta*, *ouverture*, *quodlibet*, and *aria*. In Elgar's *Enigma Variations*, each variation takes the character of one of his friends.

EXERCISES

The short piece below by the author is based on a chaconne by Henry Purcell (1659–1695). It will be used as the basis for the exercises.

EXERCISE 11-1 Make a harmonic analysis and identify nonharmonic tones.

EXERCISE 11-2 Describe in a paragraph or two the texture of each variation.

EXERCISE 11-3 Make a new variation of measures 1–8 by adding your own elaboration of the melody and bass.

***EXERCISE 11-4** Compose three more variations to be inserted before measure 25. In one of them use an ornamented version of the bass line in measures 1–8 in the top part.

CHAPTER 12

ALTERED CHORDS II
The Augmented Sixth Chords and the Neapolitan Sixth Chord

Example 12-1 Tema con variationi, Var. VII, from Piano Sonata, K 284, by W. A. Mozart (1756–1791).

Example 12-2 "Plorate, plorate, colles" from *Jefte* by Giacomo Carissimi (1605–1674).

Example 12-2 (*continued*)

Lament, lament O valleys; grieve, grieve O mountains, and in the affliction of my heart lament! Lo, I shall die a maiden, and not in my death find consolation in my children. Mourn, ye woods, meadows, and streams, in the death of a maiden, weep!

QUESTIONS FOR DISCUSSION

1. The syllables LE and FI are melodically active tones. To what syllables would you expect LE and FI to resolve? What pitches do these syllables represent in the key of D minor? in A minor?

2. What is the interval between LE and FI? When it is part of a chord, how would you expect it to resolve in the next chord?

3. Locate the appearances of chords containing LE and FI in Ex. 12-1. How do the outer voices move with respect to one another where these special chords are used? How are these chords voiced, and what other tones are included?

4. One of these chords appears in Beethoven's theme, Ex. 11-1. Is it used in any of the variations?

5. The syllable RA has a very special flavor. You have seen it as the second degree of the Phrygian mode and perhaps in a progression containing vii°7 of iv. When it is in a chord consisting of FA-LE-RA, it gains special significance. There is one in Ex. 12-1 and many instances in Ex. 12-2. Can you find them?

6. How would you expect the chord FA-LE-RA to resolve? How have Mozart and Carissimi resolved it in the examples? This chord seems to function in a manner similar to what primary chord?

THE AUGMENTED SIXTH CHORDS

The augmented sixth chords derive their name from the interval of an augmented sixth between the lowest tone and one of the upper members. Since these chords are the result of melodic motion, they do not have a functional root.

A. HARMONIC FUNCTION

    1. A preparation for the dominant or the tonic $^6_4$ in an authentic or half cadence.

    2. A pivot chord in modulation to a distantly related key.

    3. A neighboring chord (usually to the tonic).

    4. A substitute for the dominant seventh chord in an authentic cadence.

B. CONSTRUCTION: THREE TYPES ARE RECOGNIZED. ALL CONTAIN THE AUGMENTED SIXTH. GENERIC SYMBOL: A^{+6}.

    1. ITALIAN: LE-DO-FI. Symbol: It^{+6} or A^6_3. Normal doubling: DO.

    2. FRENCH: LE-DO-RE-FI. Symbol: Fr^{+6} or A^4_3.

    3. GERMAN: LE-DO-ME-FI or LE-DO-RI-FI. Symbol: Ger^{+6} or A^6_5.

    4. Most commonly used with LE as the lowest tone, but inversions are occasionally used as well. Figures for inversions are consistent with figured bass. Example: The symbol for a Fr^{+6} with DO as the lowest tone would be A^4_2.

C. RESOLUTION

   1. Regular: to the tonic triad in second inversion or to the dominant triad

      a. ITALIAN: LE to SO, DO to DO or TI, FI to SO.
      b. FRENCH: LE to SO, DO to DO or TI, RE to ME, MI or RE, FI to SO.
      c. GERMAN: LE to SO, DO to DO or TI, ME to ME or RE, FI to SO; the chord may be spelled LE-DO-RI-FI in major keys where RI resolves to MI.

Example 12-3 Regular resolutions of augmented sixth chords.

   2. Irregular

      a. The Ger^{+6} becomes a dominant seventh chord if the upper tone of the augmented sixth is spelled enharmonically. Since the Ger^{+6} can be spelled as V7 and vice versa, it can be used in modulations to remote keys. For example, in C the Ger^{+6} is A♭-C-E♭-F♯. If F♯ is spelled as G♭, we have the V7 of D♭ major. Conversely, in C the V7 is G-B-D-F. If F is spelled as E♯, we have the Ger^{+6} of B minor or major.
      b. The Fr^{+6} contains two tritones, LE-RE and DO-FI. With enharmonic spelling, the chord becomes the Fr^{+6} in a key which is a tritone distant. For example, in C the Fr^{+6} is A♭-C-D-F♯. If A♭ is spelled as G♯ and C is spelled as B♯, we have the Fr^{+6} of F♯ minor or major.
      c. The augmented sixth chords may move to a V of V before the cadence is completed.
      d. The augmented sixth chords may be used as a substitute for V7 in an authentic cadence.
      e. The augmented sixth chords may be prepared and resolved as neighboring chords.

Example 12-4 Irregular resolutions of augmented sixth chords.

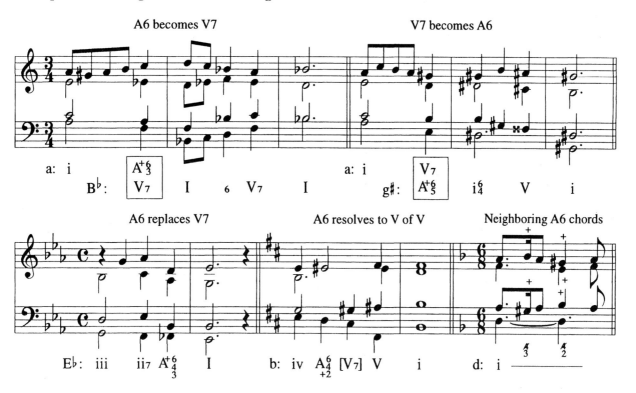

D. WHERE TO FIND THEM

1. Augmented sixth chords are more common in minor than in major keys where only one of the notes (FA to FI) must be altered. Two or three tones must be altered in major keys.

2. We perceive the interval of the augmented sixth to have a high amount of tension, and so we are likely to find it in musical moments of higher tension such as important cadences or music depicting strong emotions.

3. In Classical movements in sonata form there is often an augmented sixth chord near the end of the development.

4. Augmented sixth chords are very common in barbershop quartet harmony.

5. Augmented sixth chords figure prominently in highly chromatic passages in the music of Wagner, Franck, Tchaikovsky, and Richard Strauss.

THE NEAPOLITAN SIXTH CHORD

Composers of seventeenth-century Neapolitan opera used this chord for its emotional effect. It is normally found in first inversion, hence the name Neapolitan sixth chord. Ex. 12-2 is a particularly fine example of its use.

A. HARMONIC FUNCTION

1. A preparation for the dominant or the tonic $^6_4$ in an authentic cadence

2. A pivot chord in modulation to a distantly related key

3. A colorful substitute for the subdominant or supertonic chords

B. CONSTRUCTION

1. Major triad whose root is the lowered supertonic, usually in first inversion: FA-LE-RA. Symbol: N6. Normal doubling: FA (chord 3rd)

2. Occasionally found in other positions

   a. in root position. Symbol: N_3^5. Doubling: RA

   b. in second inversion. Symbol: N_4^6. Doubling: any member depending on context

C. RESOLUTION

1. Regular: to tonic $_4^6$, $_3^6$, or dominant

   a. FA: lowest tone; resolves to SO or ME (MI in major)
   b. LE: resolves to SO
   c. RA: usually in highest voice; resolves to DO or through TI to DO.

Example 12-5 Regular uses of the Neapolitan sixth chord.

2. Other possibilities

   a. resolves to another pre-dominant chord such as vii°⁷ of V, V of V, A⁺⁶, or VI, iv.
   b. used as pivot chord: N6 in the old key becomes a diatonic chord in the new key; a major diatonic chord in the old key becomes N6 in the new key.

Example 12-6 Other uses of the Neapolitan sixth chord.

Example 12-6 (*continued*)

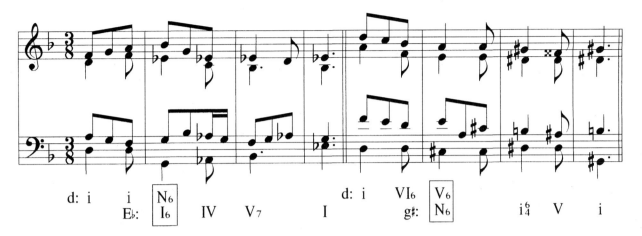

D. WHERE TO FIND THEM

1. Neapolitan sixth chords are more common in minor than in major keys where only the root tone (RE to RA) requires chromatic alteration. In major keys, the fifth (LA to LE) must be altered as well.

2. They are often used in dramatic moments for harmonic color, as exemplified in the lament from *Jefte*, Ex. 12-2.

3. Mozart and Beethoven often use them in slow movements in minor keys.

4. They can be found in chromatic music as a means of modulating to remote keys, as shown in Ex. 12-6.

EXERCISES

EXERCISE 12-1 Locate examples, one each, of the three varieties of augmented sixth chords, Italian, French and German. Copy out enough of the music to show how the chords are prepared and resolved. Draw a colored box around each augmented sixth chord, and identify it and the neighboring harmonies using roman numerals.

EXERCISE 12-2 Do the same for the Neapolitan sixth chord.

EXERCISE 12-3 Arrange this short melody for flute, oboe, and bassoon, using the given roman numerals as a guide to your harmonization.

EXERCISE 12-4 Provide alto and tenor parts for the music below, using the figured bass as a guide.

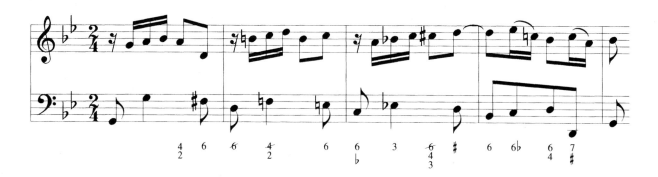

*EXERCISE 12-5 The king has written a lament and has asked you to set it to music for soprano and continuo that uses the bass of Exercise 12-4 as a ground and the melody for the first verse. We suggest a new melody for the other verses. Provide a realization for the continuo. The beginning is given below the king's lament.

THE KING'S LAMENT

With true compassion,
   Hear my lamenting,
And painful passion;
   Alas, I die.

In grief and anguish,
   My poor heart fainting,
In woe I languish.
   Alas I die.

Farewell all pleasure,
   Bereft forever;
Farewell, my treasure.
   Alas, I die.

CHAPTER 13

ALTERED CHORDS III
Third Relation, Borrowed Chords,
and Irregular Resolution

Example 13-1 "Anna, mihi dilecta," from *Altera pars selectissimarum cantionum* by Orlando di Lasso (1532–1594).

Example 13-1 (*continued*)

Anna, my beloved, come, my only delight, from whose mouth honeyed essence distills; Nymph, may you deign to give me a little kiss; in the whole world nothing else is dearer to me.

Example 13-2 Symphony No. 4 in E minor, Op. 98, Second Movement, by Johannes Brahms (1833–1897).

Example 13-2 (*continued*)

QUESTIONS FOR DISCUSSION

1. The choral work by Lasso, Ex. 13-1, is remarkably chromatic for the sixteenth century. How would you describe its texture? What chord quality and position predominates?

2. Trace the root motion throughout the piece. What is unusual about it?

3. Can you perceive a key or mode for this piece?

4. The signature for the second movement of Brahms' Fourth Symphony, Ex. 13-2, seems to indicate E Major. Brahms, however, gives us many altered scale degrees from time to time, suggesting various modes. What mode is suggested in the four-bar introduction?

5. Beginning in measure 5, E Major seems to be established, but some of the harmonies have been altered from their normal diatonic qualities. Describe these alterations in measures 5 through 8.

6. Similar alterations are used as the movement progresses. Describe others you see.

7. Examine the harmony of Chopin's Etude in E-flat minor, Op. 10 No. 6. In what unusual ways has Chopin resolved some of the dominant seventh chords and diminished seventh chords?

DEFINITIONS, PRINCIPLES, AND OBSERVATIONS

Third Relation

Harmonies are said to be in third relation when their roots are a third apart. In diatonic harmony, several third relations are possible, all of which involve two common tones between chords. Third relations involving one common tone also are common, and third relations with no common tones can be found in very chromatic music. The fewer the common tones, the more striking is the progression.

A. THIRD RELATIONS WITH TWO COMMON TONES. Note that all of these chords are diatonic, with the exception of the Neapolitan sixth chord used in minor keys.

In Major Keys			
Chord 1	**Chord 2**	**Ascending**	**Descending**
Major	Minor	I–iii, IV–vi	I–vi, IV–ii, V–iii
Minor	Major	ii–IV, iii–V, vi–I	iii–I, vi–IV

In Minor Keys			
Chord 1	**Chord 2**	**Ascending**	**Descending**
Minor	Major	i–III, iv–VI	i–VI, iv–N6, v–III
Major	Minor	N6–iv, III–v, VI–i	III–i, VI–iv

B. THIRD RELATIONS WITH ONE COMMON TONE. Note that most of the examples involve secondary dominants.

Chord 1	Chord 2	Ascending Examples	Descending Examples
Major	Major	*By major third:* In major: I–V/vi, IV–V/ii, V–V/iii, ♭VII–V/V In minor: III–V, VI–V/iv	*By major third:* In major: I–♭VI, IV–N6, V–♭III, V/VI–I In minor: IV–N6, V–III, V/iv–VI
Major	Major	*By minor third:* In major: I–♭III, IV–♭VI, V–♭VII, V/V–IV, V/vi–V In minor: IV–VI, V–♭VII, ♭VII–N6	*By minor third:* In major: I–V/ii, IV–V/V, V–V/vi, ♭VII–V; In minor: III–V/iv, IV–V/V, VI–IV
Minor	Minor	*By major third:* A minor to C♯ minor, C minor to E minor, F minor to A minor	*By minor third:* C minor to A minor E minor to C♯ minor, G minor to E minor

C. THIRD RELATIONS WITH NO COMMON TONES. Note that these chord relationships tend to obscure the tonality.

Chord 1	Chord 2	Ascending Examples	Descending Examples
Major	Minor	*By minor third:* C major to E♭ minor, D major to F minor, B major to D minor	*By major third:* E major to C minor, A major to F minor, F♯ major to D minor
Minor	Major	*By major third:* C minor to E major, F minor to A major, B♭ minor to D major	*By minor third:* G minor to E major, D minor to B major, C minor to A major

D. DOMINANT SEVENTH CHORDS MAY BE USED IN THIRD RELATION

    1. Examples with root movement by minor third: C7 to A7, F7 to D7, B♭7 to G7, D♭7 to B♭7

    2. Examples with root movement by major third: G7 to B7, C7 to E7, F♯7 to D7, C♯7 to A7

    3. Root movement by minor third is smooth, since there will be two common tones.

    4. Root movement by major third is striking, since there will be only one common tone.

E. VOICE LEADING AND DOUBLING

    1. Common tones are generally retained.

    2. Stepwise motion is generally used, especially in the higher voices.

    3. Both chords are normally in root position; the bass moves by thirds.

    4. Although root position is the norm, inversions of one or both chords are possible.

Example 13-3 Third relations in various contexts.

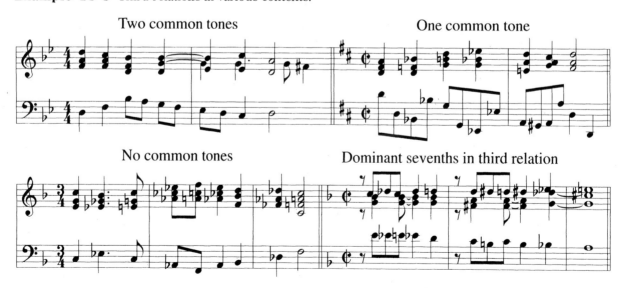

Borrowed Chords

Composers can add color to the harmony by altering the quality of diatonic chords or by "borrowing" chords from the parallel key. Tones most often altered are the third, sixth, and seventh scale degrees. Use of these chords results in a kind of "modal mixture." The term *chord mutation* also is used to describe borrowed chords.

A. IN MINOR KEYS

1. Picardy Third. The third of the tonic triad is raised, changing it from minor to major. It is most often found in final cadences, but it may occur elsewhere.

2. Major IV. The normal quality of the subdominant is minor, but the major IV may be used in response to the ascending form of the melodic minor (SO-LA-TI-DO). It gives a Dorian modal flavor to the music.

3. Minor v. The normal quality of the dominant is major, but the minor v may be used in response to the descending form of the melodic minor, DO-TE-LE-SO. It is sometimes called "the modal dominant."

4. Other borrowed chords are ii and ii7 (raised 5th) and ♭VII (lowered root).

Example 13-4 Borrowed chords in the minor mode.

B. IN MAJOR KEYS

1. Minor iv. The third of the IV chord is lowered, changing it from major to minor (equivalent to "borrowing" the subdominant from the parallel minor key).

2. Full diminished vii°7. When the sixth degree of the scale is lowered in a vii7, the chord becomes a fully diminished seventh chord, a very effective dominant function chord.

3. Major ♭VI and ♭III. These chords are borrowed from the parallel minor for the sake of added harmonic color and can be used to give a modal flavor to the music. They can be very useful in modulation to remote keys.

4. The lowered ♭VII. When the root of the vii triad is lowered, the quality becomes major. It lends a Mixolydian flavor to the harmony.

5. The V⁺. Raising the fifth of the dominant triad creates a colorful sonority that resolves to the tonic with two strong leading-tones, TI-DO and RI-MI.

6. Other borrowed chords are the v (see Ex. 13-2, measures 7–8) and the ii⌀7 (lowered fifth).

Example 13-5 Borrowed chords in the major mode.

F: I   iv♭ vii°⁴₃   ♭III   ♭VI [V₇]   IV   V⁺   I   ii°⁴₂   I

Irregular Resolution of Dominant Seventh Chords and Diminished Seventh Chords

Dominant seventh chords and diminished seventh chords normally resolve to tonic chords in both major and minor keys. Other resolutions are possible, however, and are referred to as "irregular resolutions." Diminished seventh chords are unique in that all chord members are three semitones apart from one another, making a determination of chord position or inversion by ear impossible until a resolution is heard. When a diminished seventh chord is respelled enharmonically, many alternate resolutions become possible.

A. IRREGULAR RESOLUTION OF DOMINANT SEVENTH CHORDS

1. The deceptive progressions. V–vi in major keys and V–VI in minor keys are the most common. Other possibilities include V7–♭VI, V7–vii°7/V, and V7–iii.

2. Resolution by third relation (see Ex. 13-6)

3. Resolution as German augmented sixth chords to a remote key (see Ex. 12-4 and Ex. 13-6)

4. One or more of the tones in the dominant seventh chord moves up or down a semitone, creating a new sonority. Examples: SO moves to LE, creating a diminished seventh chord; TI moves to TE, creating a minor-minor seventh chord; RE moves to RA, creating a French augmented sixth chord; FA moves to MI, creating a minor-minor seventh chord.

Example 13-6 Irregular resolutions of dominant seventh chords.

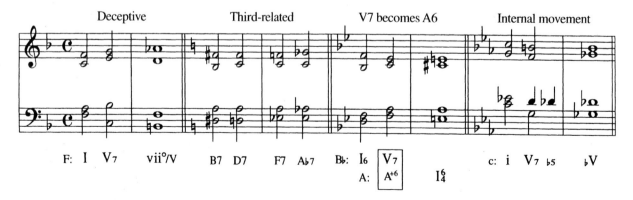

F: I   V₇   vii°/V   B7   D7   F7   A♭7   B♭: I₆   V₇   c: i   V₇ ♭5   ♭V

A: A⁺⁶   I⁶₄

B. IRREGULAR RESOLUTION OF DIMINISHED SEVENTH CHORDS

> **1.** Any chord member can be lowered, producing a dominant seventh chord. Examples: Beginning with the pitches G♯-B-D-F, if F is lowered to E, the result is an E7 chord; if the G♯ is lowered to G, the result is a G7 chord; if B is lowered to B♭ and G♯ is spelled as A♭, the result is a B♭7 chord; if the D is lowered to C♯ and the F is spelled as E♯, the result is a C♯7 chord.
>
> **2.** With an enharmonic spelling, any chord member can become the leading tone. Examples: Beginning with the pitches G♯-B-D-F, the G♯ would be the normal leading tone; if the chord is spelled A♭-B-D-F, B becomes the leading tone; if it is spelled as A♭-C♭-D-F, D becomes the leading tone; if it is spelled as G♯-B-D-E♯, E♯ becomes the leading tone.
>
> **3.** A diminished seventh chord can resolve as a "Neighboring °7," where one of its tones becomes the root of the major or minor triad that resolves it. Examples: C-D♯-F♯-A resolving to C-E-G (C is the common tone, D♯-F♯-A are neighbor tones); F-A♭-B-D resolving to F-A♭-C (B and D are neighbor tones)
>
> **4.** Any diminished seventh chord may move to a different diminished seventh chord.

Example 13-7 Irregular resolutions of diminished seventh chords.

Lowering a chord tone   New leading tone

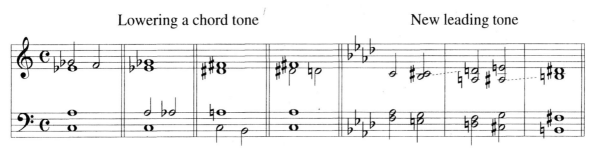

Neighboring diminished seventh chords   Dim. 7 to another Dim. 7

EXERCISES   **EXERCISE 13-1** Complete the piano accompaniment.

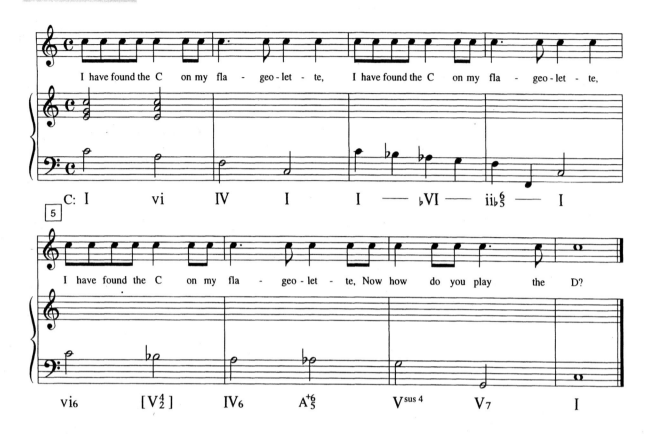

EXERCISE 13-2 The regular resolution for a D7 chord is a G chord. Name five irregular resolutions for a D7 chord.

EXERCISE 13-3 Below is a simplified version of the first sixteen measures of Etude Op. 10, No. 6 by Chopin. Make a harmonic analysis, and write a paragraph discussing irregular resolutions it contains.

EXERCISE 13-4 Below is an arrangement of a familiar barbershop quartet tune. Locate each chord in the following list by writing its number in a circle below the score in the appropriate place. The first two chords have been done for you as an example.

1. ii_5^6 (or IV with added 6th) [m. 35]

2. French A6 to V of V [m. 12]

3. Neighboring $°7$ to I_6

4. German A6 to I_4^6 with added 6th (vii_2^4)

5. $vii°_2^4$ of V to V_3^4

6. German A6 in $_2^4$ position to ii_7

7. Neighboring $° \; _5^6$ to V_3^4

8. V7 of V to V7

9. Neighboring $° \; _5^6$ to V_3^4

10. French A6 to V of ii

11. $ii_{7♭}5$ (borrowed chord)

12. V7 of vi to vi

EXERCISE 13-5 Complete the piano accompaniment for this short tenor aria in the style of Rossini. Make use of some third related chords, borrowed chords, and irregular resolutions.

CHAPTER 14

MODULATION—LARGER FORMS

Example 14-1 Scherzo from Quartet, Op. 18 No. 1 by Ludwig van Beethoven (1770–1827).

Allegro molto

Example 14-1 (*continued*)

Example 14-1 (*continued*)

QUESTIONS FOR DISCUSSION

1. Although the Scherzo clearly begins and ends in F Major, Beethoven manages to move through and modulate to several closely related keys and a few more distantly related ones. What are they, and where are they established?

2. What triads do F Major and C Major have in common? What chords does Beethoven use for the *pivot* in the modulation established at the end of the first strain?

3. For the primary thematic material, Beethoven employs a modulating sequence. Make a chord analysis of measures 1–6. How does this compare with later presentations in measures 37–46 and 64–70?

DEFINITIONS, PRINCIPLES, AND OBSERVATIONS

Modulation

Change of key is an essential aspect of Western music from the earliest times, and it is a trait that distinguishes it from musics of many other cultures. Below is a summary of principles of key change in tonal music, which we call *modulation*, and some commonly used terms associated with it.

A. DEFINITIONS OF TERMS

   1. *Modulation* is a process used by the composer to move from one key to another.

   2. The term *pivot* is often used to describe the place in the music where a move toward the new key becomes possible. The chord preceding accidentals often serves as a pivot, since it can function in either the original key or the new key. Chords that can function in both the old and new keys are called *common chords*.

   3. The term *modulatory* is used to describe music where there is a series of key changes, none of which is firmly established; the tonal focus is transitory. Development sections and transitions often employ modulatory passages.

   4. The term *remodulation* is sometimes used to denote modulation from a secondary key back to the original key.

B. PERMANENCE OF THE KEY CHANGE. Modulation procedures are used for three *degrees of permanence.*

   1. The brief emphasis of a scale degree other than the tonic. This is referred to as movement to or within a *region.* In Ex. 14-1, measure 2, beat 3 through measure 4, beat 2, the key of G minor is suggested—the region of ii (the supertonic) is emphasized. Measure 4, beat 3 through measure 6 emphasize the region of iii (the mediant). Measures 7 through 10 establish the region of V (the dominant).

   2. The temporary establishment of a new key in small forms such as the rounded binary or in sections of a larger work. In Ex. 14-1, the key of A♭ is established at the beginning of the second strain (measure 11 through measure 18).

   3. The more permanent establishment of a new key area in larger forms such as sonata-allegro and rondo forms. In the first movement of Schubert's Symphony No. 8 ("Unfinished"), the opening is in the key of B minor. The second theme firmly establishes the key of G Major.

   4. Modulation may or may not involve a change of key signature depending on the relationship and permanence of the new key.

C. KEY RELATIONSHIPS. Change of key may occur from any key to any other key. It is useful, however, to consider two *degrees of key change*:

1. *Closely related keys* consist of the relative minor or major keys, the tonic major or minor keys, and keys whose signatures have one more or one less sharp or flat. For example, keys which are considered closely related to F Major are D minor, F minor, B♭ Major, F minor, C Major, and A minor.

2. *Distantly related keys* or *remote keys* consist of all keys other than the closely related keys. For example, D Major and A♭ minor are considered distantly related keys.

D. REQUIREMENTS FOR SMOOTH MODULATION. The following three musical events are normally encountered in the process of modulation:

1. The *establishment of the original key*—sufficient music for a key to be perceived.

2. The presentation of *music that can be perceived as "belonging" to both the original key and the new key*. This music may be a single note, a single harmony, or a group of harmonies. This is usually referred to as the *pivot*.

3. The *establishment of the new key*—sufficient music for the new key to be perceived. This is usually accomplished by a strong cadence.

E. TYPES OF MODULATION. Modulation may be accomplished in the following ways:

1. By *common chord* or *chords*. Chords are used that have a harmonic identity in both the original and new keys. Examples: F-A-C is the tonic in F Major and the dominant in B♭ Major; D-F♯-A is the subdominant in A Major and V of V in C Major.

2. By *enharmonic common chord*. When a chord in one key has a harmonic identity in another key if enharmonic spelling is used, it may function as a common chord. Example: B-D-F-A♭ is vii°7 in C minor; and if G♯ is used instead of A♭, the chord becomes viig in first inversion in the key of A minor.

3. By *common note*. A note in one key that has a different diatonic (or melodic) identity in another key may be used as a pivot. The note is featured prominently (sometimes sounded alone) before its new context is provided. In Ex. 14-1, measure 10, the note C functions as the tonic. In measure 11, C is the mediant of A♭ Major.

4. By *chromatic alteration*. A member of a chord (often the third) in the original key is raised or lowered, changing the *color* of the chord so that it can be used as a pivot to a new key. The passage in measures 25 through 36 in Ex. 14-1 appears to be in the key of F minor, but the harmony in measure 37 returns to F Major by raising the chord third.

5. By *modulating sequence*. A set of harmonies is restated in one or more sequences ending with a cadence in a new key. The sequence beginning in measure 17, Ex. 14-1 continues through measure 23, where the key of F minor is established.

6. By *suspension of the tonality*. Music is presented that results in tonal ambiguity, then a strong cadence is provided that establishes a key. Modulatory passages in development sections of chromatic music make use of this technique.

7. By *brute force*. A new key (often a remote one) is presented with no preparation. This often involves dramatic changes in texture and dynamics.

Larger Forms

The articulation of form is dependent upon key scheme as well as thematic content and changes in texture. This is especially true in the larger forms developed in the Classical era. Below is a summary of the essential structural elements of several larger forms.

A. FORMS BASED ON THE TERNARY SCHEME

1. *Da capo aria.* Scheme: A–B–A′, in which A represents the main musical idea of the aria presented in the tonic key, B represents a contrasting section in a closely related key, and A′ represents a repetition of the A material in which the soloist performs an ornamented version of the melody. The ornamentation, if not actually improvised, is improvisational in character.

2. *Minuet and trio.* Both the minuet and the trio consist of two strains, each repeated. In performance the minuet is played, then the trio, then the minuet is played again omitting the repeats. The scheme of the minuet is ‖: A :‖: B A′ :‖. A is often a single period, which sometimes modulates to the dominant or relative major. B begins with new material or material related to the A idea in the new key, modulates back to the tonic, and ends with a half cadence. A′ is a varied repetition of A and does not modulate. A short coda may be added. The trio follows the same scheme with its own thematic ideas, is usually less dramatic than the minuet, and may be somewhat shorter in length.

3. *Scherzo and trio.* The plan is the same as the minuet and trio, except that the tempo is considerably faster, and instead of the B that begins the second strain, a short, modulatory development of the A material appears. Ex. 14-1 is typical of the form. The term *scherzo* is used as well in a broader sense for pieces of a playful character and quick tempo.

B. SONATA FORMS

1. The structure of sonata form is basically an enlargement of binary form. The first part contains the exposition, which is usually repeated. The second part contains the development section and recapitulation. This part was generally repeated until the late eighteenth century.

    a. The *exposition* introduces the thematic material of the movement. The primary thematic material is presented in the tonic, and the secondary thematic material is presented in a new key, usually the dominant or relative major. A transition is normally used as a means of modulating from the tonic to the new key. Thematic material of a conclusive character is often used to end the exposition (the "closing theme"). Larger sonata movements may begin with an introduction preceding the presentation of the primary thematic material.

    b. The *development* section presents the thematic material of the exposition (most often the primary material) in varied ways and is modulatory, touching upon keys more distantly related than the key established at the end of the exposition. After reaching a climax, the development modulates back to the tonic in preparation for the recapitulation.

    c. The *recapitulation* presents the thematic material of the exposition, except that the transition ends in the tonic instead of the new key. The secondary thematic material now appears in the tonic. If the original key is minor, a shift to the tonic major often occurs for the secondary thematic material. A coda may be used to end the movement. In Beethoven's larger sonata-form movements, the coda may rival the development in length.

2. When the word sonata is used to indicate a classical genre, it refers to a multimovement work for solo instrument or for an instrument with piano. During the Baroque era, sonata was simply a composition in one or more movements for instrumental solo or ensemble.

3. Sonata form is usually used for the opening movement (and occasionally the closing movement) of sonatas, symphonies, concertos, and chamber works such as trios, quartets, quintets, and so on.

4. During the Classical era, the opening movement of a concerto used a "double exposition" in which the orchestra presents the thematic material before the entrance of the solo, which presents the material in a varied form. A cadenza was usually played before the closing material. In early concertos the cadenza was improvised, but by the middle of the nineteenth century, it was written out by the composer.

5. Sonatina form is a miniature sonata form. It may present all of the sections of a sonata movement, but in compact form; it may have the dimensions of a sonata form, but omit the development section; it may be monothematic, having no secondary thematic material.

C. RONDO FORMS

1. Rondo forms consist of a primary theme that alternates with one or more secondary themes. The simplest structure has five parts with the scheme: A–B–A–C–A, where A is the primary theme, often referred to as "the rondo." B and C are new themes.

2. The primary theme may be shortened, varied, or treated to some kind of development in its later presentations.

3. The B theme is usually presented in the dominant. In the simple form shown above, the C theme is usually in the subdominant or some other closely related key.

4. A larger rondo form has the scheme: A–B–A–C–A–B–A. The C section shows the highest contrast to either the A or B themes. It may be in a remote key, it may be modulatory, or it may consist of passage-work with little melodic content.

5. The final presentation of the A theme is often coda-like.

6. Some other rondo schemes are: A–B–A–B'–A and A–B–A–C–B–A.

7. Rondo forms are often used as the final movement for sonatas, symphonies, concertos, and multimovement chamber works.

D. SONATA-RONDO

1. When sonata and rondo elements are used together, the result is called sonata-rondo form. It is most often found as the closing movement in larger Classical works.

2. A common scheme is: A–B–A–Development–A–B'–A–Coda. The sonata form elements are the contrasting themes, development, and recapitulation with the B' in the tonic key. The rondo element is the recurrance of the A theme after each digression.

E. FUGUE

1. Fugue is more properly considered a genre than a form, since it has no fixed structure. In a fugue a theme or subject is exposed and then developed.

2. Exposition:

   a. The subject is presented first by one of the voices in the tonic key. A second voice then presents the subject in the dominant key while the first voice continues with counterpoint.
   b. A third voice then enters, again in the tonic, and the first and second voices continue in counterpoint.
   c. If there is a fourth voice, it enters next, again in the dominant, the other voices continuing with counterpoint. If there are more than four voices, the process continues as above.
   d. A short "bridge" may appear between entries in order to modulate to the key required by the next entrance.
   e. If the counterpoint provided by the first voice to the entrance of the second is used by other voices when they accompany the subject, that contrapuntal material is called a countersubject.
   f. In large fugues, the exposition may be repeated but with a different order of voice entries. Counterpoint continues in the other voices.

3. Development

   a. The subject appears from time to time in any of the voices during the development. These occurrances are called "middle entries."
   b. The composer has the choice of a number of options in the development.

      i) The subject may be presented in various keys, including changes of mode from major to minor or vice versa.
      ii) The subject may be melodically inverted.
      iii) The subject may be presented in *stretto*: one voice presents the subject, and another voice enters with the subject before the first voice has completed its presentation. Stretto may involve two or more voices.
      iv) A middle entry may present the subject with notes of smaller time values, called *diminution*, or larger time values, called *augmentation*.
      v) Passages in the development that do not contain any complete subject entries are called "episodes." They often contain sequences and modulation.

   c. In order to reestablish the tonic key for the close of the fugue, composers often employ a pedal point on the dominant.
   d. The final subject entries emphasize the tonic key. A tonic pedal is used occasionally to emphasize the tonic in the closing bars.

4. Special types of fugues include:

   a. Double or triple fugues that contain two or three subjects.
   b. Choral fugato, a fugal chorus that may or may not be accompanied. Anthems and motets may be fugal in nature. Choruses from masses, cantatas, and oratorios are often fugal.
   c. Masked fugue, a fugue with continuous accompaniment figures that do not participate in the presentation of the subject.

EXERCISES

EXERCISE 14-1 Harmonize this chorale melody in four parts. The final note of each phrase is traditionally marked with a fermata (⌢). Phrase 1 establishes the tonic, Phrase 2 modulates to the dominant, Phrase 3 modulates to the supertonic, and Phrase 4 remodulates to the tonic. Use common-chord modulations. Provide a chord analysis.

EXERCISE 14-2 Locate a minuet, scherzo, or trio from a string quartet by Haydn that modulates to a closely related key in the first strain. Make a photocopy of it, then take a colored pen and make a chord analysis showing the harmonies in the original key, the pivot harmony (or harmonies), and the harmonies that establish the new key.

EXERCISE 14-3 Below is the antecedent phrase of a period and at a) a sample consequent phrase that modulates to B minor. At b) and c) write consequent phrases that modulate respectively to C Major and D Major. Provide a chord analysis for each.

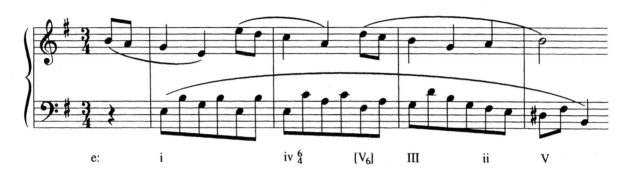

e: i   iv $^6_4$ [V$_6$]   III   ii   V

a) Sample consequent phrase that modulates to B minor

e: i
b: iv   V^7 i   iv   V   i

b) Consequent phrase that modulates to C major

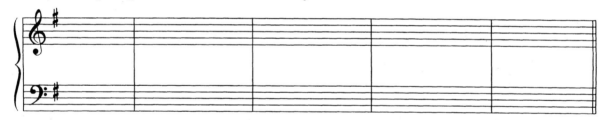

c) Consequent phrase that modulates to D major

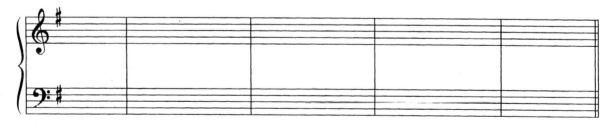

*EXERCISE 14-4 Describe the modulation procedures used to reach each of the keys indicated below the score beginning in measure 5. Name the type of modulation and explain how it is achieved.

*EXERCISE 14-5 Write a sequence that modulates up by major third. Continue until it arrives at the original key an octave higher. Write another sequence that modulates down by whole step until it reaches an octave below.

*EXERCISE 14-6 Analyze this short fugue showing all subject entrances. Indicate any instances of episodes, subject inversion, and stretto. Indicate the key scheme and modulations.

CHAPTER 15

EXTENDED CHORDS, ADDED TONES, AND JAZZ HARMONY

Example 15-1 "Le jardin féerique" from *Ma Mére L'oye* for piano, four hands by Maurice Ravel (1875–1937).

Example 15-1 (*continued*)

Example 15-1 (*continued*)

Example 15-2 Lead sheet for "Autumn Leaves," music by Joseph Kosma, harmonization by the author. (Autumn Leaves (Les Feuilles Mortes). English lyric by Johnny Mercer, French lyric by Jacques Prevert, Music by Joseph Kosma © 1947, 1950 (renewed) ENOCH ET CIE. Sole selling agent for U. S. and Canada: MORLEY MUSIC CO., by arrangement with ENOCH ET CIE. All Rights Reserved.)

QUESTIONS FOR DISCUSSION

1. Triads are made by stacking up two thirds. Seventh chords are made by stacking up three thirds. If you stack up four thirds, what interval do you have between the root and the highest note?

2. Continuing in the same manner, what results from a stack of five thirds? six thirds? If you have a stack of seven thirds using white keys beginning on C, what is the pitch of the highest note?

3. The chord on the third beat of measure 20, Ex. 15-1 has five different pitch classes. Arrange them into a stack of thirds. What is the quality of the triad at the bottom? The lower four notes of the stack form what type of seventh chord? What is the interval from the lowest pitch to the highest?

4. The harmonies in measures 1 through 10 in Ex. 15-1 have just four parts. Some of them are triads, and some are seventh chords. Still others appear to be ninth chords. Which chord members have been omitted in the ninth chords?

5. Example 7-1 includes many rich sonorities. Try to locate some ninth chords and thirteenth chords.

6. Look at the first chord in measure 4, Ex. 15-1. It appears to be a C Major triad, but the A in the top part seems to be a chord member rather than a nonharmonic tone. It does not function as the root of an A minor seventh chord. How can we account for it?

7. The series of chords beginning in measure 35, Ex. 7-1 contains several triads with a sixth added above the root, and some are seventh chords. How would you indicate each chord using lead-sheet symbols?

8. What notes are indicated by the chord symbols in Ex. 15-2? in Ex. 1-2?

DEFINITIONS, PRINCIPLES, AND OBSERVATIONS

Extended Chords

Tertian harmony is based on chord structures made of thirds. We have seen how triads and seventh chords are constructed by superimposing major and minor thirds. Extended chords continue the process to include ninth chords, eleventh chords, and thirteenth chords. The upper tones give the chords added color.

A. NINTH CHORDS

1. A ninth appearing above a dominant seventh chord as a suspension or an appoggiatura has been in use since the Baroque period. Later the ninth could be considered as a member of the chord.

2. As with the appoggiatura, the ninth resolves down by step.

3. The fifth of the chord may be omitted.

4. When a ninth appears above a triad (without a seventh), it functions as an added second (see chords with "Added Tones" below).

TYPES OF NINTH CHORDS

Quality of Seventh chord	Extension Interval	Chord Function in C Major or Minor	Lead Sheet Symbol	Essential Pitches	Optional Pitch
M-M7	M9	C: I^9 C: IV^9	CM9 FM9	C-E-B-D F-A-E-G	G C
M-m7	M9	C: V^9	G9	G-B-F-A	D
M-m7	m9	c: V^9	G7($\flat$9)	G-B-F-A$\flat$	D
m-m7	M9	C: ii^9 C: vi^9	Dm9 Am9	D-F-C-E A-C-G-B	A E
dim-m7	M9	c: ii$^{\o}$9	D$^{\o}$(9)	D-F-A$\flat$-C-E	—

B. ELEVENTH CHORDS

1. The tonic note appearing as a suspension or an appoggiatura above a dominant seventh chord is a perfect eleventh above the bass. It resolves to the leading tone. If this tone is not resolved while the dominant seventh is active, it is considered the eleventh of a dominant eleventh chord.

2. An eleventh chord may occur as a IV or ii^7 above a dominant pedal.

3. If the eleventh does not resolve down, it may be repeated, retained, or move to a chord tone in the next harmony.

4. The eleventh replaces the third of a dominant eleventh chord (the third is omitted).

5. When the eleventh is augmented, the third is used and the fifth is omitted.

6. The augmented eleventh is sometimes spelled enharmically as a lowered fifth ($\flat$5) and may resolve down (see Ex. 15-3, measure 16).

TYPES OF ELEVENTH CHORDS

Quality of Seventh chord	Extension Interval	Chord Function in C Major or Minor	Lead Sheet Symbol	Essential Pitches	Optional Pitches
M-m7	P11	C: V^{11}	G sus 4 or G7(11) or F/G	G-D-F-C	A, A♭
M-m7	+11	C: V^{+11}	G7(+11)	G-B-F-C♯	A, A♭
m-m7	P11	C: ii^{11} c: vi^{11}	Dm7(11) Am7(11)	D-F-C-G A-C-G-D	A, E E, B

C. THIRTEENTH CHORDS

1. A suspension or appoggiatura that resolves to the fifth above a dominant seventh chord is the predecessor of the dominant thirteenth chord. Chopin, Schumann, and other composers of the Romantic period often used a thirteenth that did not resolve while the dominant seventh was active (see Ex. 15-3).

2. The thirteenth replaces the fifth of a dominant seventh chord (the fifth is omitted).

3. A dominant thirteenth chord may be enriched by the addition of a ninth or augmented eleventh.

4. When a thirteenth appears above a triad (without a seventh), it functions as an added sixth (see chords with "Added Tones" below).

TYPES OF THIRTEENTH CHORDS

Quality of Seventh chord	Extension Interval	Chord Function in C Major or Minor	Lead Sheet Symbol	Essential Pitches	Optional Pitches
M-m7	M13	C: V^{13}	G7(13)	G-B-F-E	A, A♭, C♯
M-m7	m13	c: V^{13}	G7(♭13)	G-B-F-E♭	A, A♭

Example 15-3 Extended chords in Mazurka, Op. 24, No. 4 , measures 13–20 by Frédérick Chopin (1810–1849).

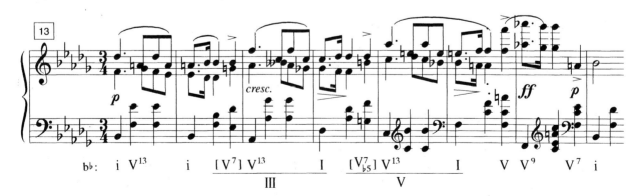

In the example above, the thirteenths in measures 13 and 17 are minor, the thirteenth in measure 15 is major, and the ninth in measure 19 is minor. The $V^7_{\flat 5}$ chord in measure 16 is equivalent to an inverted French augmented sixth chord.

Chords with Added Tones

Harmonies can be made more colorful by the addition of tones. The major sixth added to a major triad appeared first as a minor-minor seventh chord in first inversion. In the late nineteenth century, composers began to add a sixth to triads other than the subdominant. By the time of Debussy and Ravel, chords with added major or minor sixth and added major or minor second were quite common. A dominant seventh chord with added minor third (or augmented ninth) is common in jazz and "blues" harmony.

A. ADDED SIXTH

1. The major triad with added major sixth. This chord is most commonly found on I or IV in major keys, but it may be found on III or VI in minor keys as well.

2. The major triad with added minor sixth. This chord has an exotic flavor and is found in the works of French and Spanish composers around the turn of the century.

3. The minor triad with added major sixth. This chord is rather dark in color and is often used to evoke the feeling of mystery or danger.

4. The minor triad with minor sixth. This chord is somewhat rare and is easily confused with a major-major seventh chord in first inversion.

5. Adding a sixth to a triad does not change the harmonic function of the triad.

6. In roman numeral nomenclature a chord consisting of C-E-G-A in the key of G may be indicated either as ii^6_5 or IV^{add6}. In lead sheet notation it is indicated by C6.

7. Added sixth chords may include the added second as well. A triad with added major sixth and major second contains all of the tones of the pentatonic scale.

B. ADDED SECOND

1. Major triad with added major second. The added tone thickens and colors the sonority.

2. Major triad with added minor second. This chord has a pungent flavor associated with Flamenco music. Ravel and Debussy frequently use this sonority to invoke Spanish images.

3. Minor triad with added major or minor second. These chords are used mainly as clusters. The triadic quality is somewhat obscured.

4. Adding a second to a triad does not change the harmonic function of the triad.

5. In roman numeral nomenclature a chord consisting of C-D-E-G in the key of G may be indicated as IV^{add2}. In lead sheet notation it may be indicated as CM9.

Example 15-4 Added-tone chords in Debussy's piano music: a. From "Golliwogg's cake walk." b. From "La fille aux cheveux de lin."

a) Triads with added seconds   b) Triads with added sixths

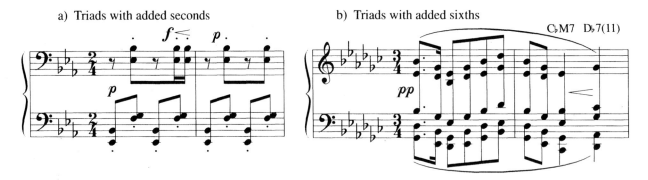

C. ADDED MINOR THIRD

1. This chord consists of a dominant seventh with a minor third added above the seventh. Example: C–E–G–B♭–E♭

2. The minor third is sometimes spelled enharmonically as an augmented ninth.

3. Because of its striking quality, it is often referred to as "the sting chord" in jazz circles.

4. In lead sheet notation it may be indicated as C7(♭3) or C7(+9).

Example 15-5 The dominant seventh with added minor third used in a sequence with thirteenth chords.

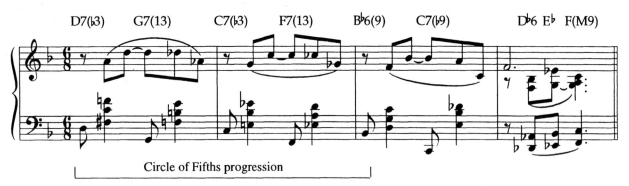

Note that the first chord in measure 3 is a stack of perfect fourths and contains all of the pitches in a pentatonic collection.

Jazz Harmony

The information presented here is a brief summary of harmonic principles and conventions used by jazz musicians in improvisation and arranging for solo, combo, and larger jazz ensembles.

A. CHORD VOCABULARY. Labeling and spelling of chords in jazz harmony is for ease in communicating the desired pitches, not for theoretical correctness. Because chord symbols have never been standardized, a particular chord may be indicated in several ways.

   NOTE: In the outline below, measure numbers in parentheses refer to Ex. 15-2.

1. Although all qualities of triads are used, sevenths are generally added for harmonic color.

    a. Dominant function chords nearly always include the minor seventh (measures 6, 14, 18, 26, 30).
    b. Major sevenths can be added to major triads (measures 3, 4, 28) and minor sevenths can be added to minor triads (measure 1, 21).
    c. A major seventh can be added to a minor triad, which is usually treated as an appoggiatura (measures 7, 15, 19).
    d. Minor sevenths may be added to diminished triads to create half-diminished chords (measures 5, 25, 29). A half-diminished seventh chord may be indicated as a minor seventh chord with lowered fifth (F♯-A-C-E may be indicated as F♯dim(m7), F♯ø7 or F♯m7(♭5).
    e. Diminished sevenths may be added to diminished triads to create full diminished seventh chords (see Ex. 1-2, mm. 14).

2. A major sixth is often added to major triads (measure 24), and occasionally to minor triads (measures 8, 20). The minor added sixth is rare.

3. Dominant seventh chords often are enriched by the addition of ninths, elevenths, or thirteenths (measures 2, 14, 22, 26, 30). These extensions may be diatonic or altered, and they may be used in various combinations.

4. Chords are most often indicated in root position. An inversion can be shown, however, using a slash after the symbol followed by the pitch to be used in the bass (measure 27). The symbol Emin/G indicates an E minor triad in first inversion (with G in the bass).

5. Slash notation is used for a chord with a bass pitch that is not a member of the chord (measure 21). Spelled from the bottom up, the sonority D–C–E–G–A can be indicated by the symbol C6/D.

6. A chord constructed of a perfect fifth and perfect fourth above the root is common in jazz harmony (measures 17, 30). A chord consisting of C–F–G is given the symbol Csus4. The "suspended fourth" may or may not resolve as expected in "classical music."

7. The "sting chord," consisting of a dominant seventh with a minor third added above the seventh, is a sonority that comes from "the blues." The flatted or "bent" third is one of the characteristic "blue notes." As mentioned above, the minor third may appear spelled enharmonically as an augmented ninth (see Ex. 15-5, mm. 1, 2).

8. A chord that came into use in "bee-bop" and "cool jazz" styles is the dominant seventh chord with flatted fifth (or the augmented eleventh). C7(♭5) would be spelled C-E-B♭-G♭. Such a chord might also include a D or D♭ as well.

9. The *fourth chord*—a stack of two or more perfect fourths—is often used in contemporary jazz (see Ex. 15-5, measure 3).

B. COMMON JAZZ CHORD PROGRESSIONS AND PATTERNS

1. *The Blues.* Early blues singers used a simple progression of twelve bars in length with a dominant in bar 12 that prepares for repetitions. The last repetition ends on the tonic. The traditional blues progression is shown here in C Major. Number 1 shows the ending for all repetitions but the last. Number 2 shows the final ending. The two chords shown in the next-to-last bar receive two beats each.

| C | F7 | C | C7 | F7 | F7 | C | C | G7 | F7 |¹ C | G7 :‖
‖² C–G7 | C ‖

As jazz musicians used the blues progression for instrumental improvisation, a more varied progression evolved. The harmonic rhythm in the final ending is: | ♩ ♩ ♩ ♩ | ♩ ♫ ♩ 𝄾 ‖

| C6 | F7 | C6 | C7 | F7 | F7 | C6–Dm7 | Em7–E♭m7|
| Dm7–G7 | Dm7–G7 ‖¹ C6–E♭°7 | Dm7–G7 :‖
‖² C6–C7/E–F6–F♯°7 | C/G–D♭7–C7‖

In the late 1940s, the great jazz saxophonist Charlie Parker developed a version of the blues progression that was much more varied:

C6–F7 | Bm7–E7 | Am7–D7(♭5) | Gm7–C7(♭5) | Cm7–F7 |
| Fm7–B♭7 | Em7 | A7(♭5) | Dm7–G7 | Dm7–G7 ‖¹ C6–E♭M7 |
| A♭M7–G7 :‖² C6–D♭7 | C7(♭5)‖

2. *Circle of Fifths.* Popular songs and jazz tunes use Circle of Fifths progressions extensively. The chord roots trace a sequence of falling perfect fifths (or rising perfect fourths).

   a. The chord sequence may be diatonic, as in Ex. 15-2 (root triads are: iv–VII–III–VI–ii°–V–i). The familiar song, "All the things you are" begins in a similar fashion, but in the major (vi–ii–V–I).

   b. The chord sequence may be a series of dominant-related chords, as in Ex. 15-5 (each chord has a dominant relationship to the next). The old tunes "Sweet Georgia Brown" and "Lulu's back in town" begin with a "cascade" of dominant-related chords.

3. *Step progressions.* Root movement involving rising or falling steps is common in jazz harmony. Examples in C Major: CM7–Dm7–Em7–E♭°7–Dm7 and FM7–Em7–Dm7–D♭7–CM7.

4. *Half-step progressions.* Root movement in ascending or descending half steps also is common. Examples: C6–C♯°7–Dm7–D♭°7–Em7 and G7–F♯7–F7–E7. The beginning of the old tune "Liza" is often harmonized by chords with roots ascending in half steps.

C. CHORD SUBSTITUTION AND HARMONIC ELABORATION. In order to create variety and color in harmonization, jazz musicians can substitute a given chord with another. They can add smoothness and motion to the harmony by using embellishing chords between the essential ones.

1. Chord substitution

   a. *Change of chord quality.* A chord with the same root but a different quality of triad, seventh, extensions, or added tones may be substituted for the original chord as long as there is no interference with the melody note. In Ex. 15-2, measure 23, GM9 is used instead of G6 to provide tension and harmonic motion.

   b. *Third-related chords.* Chords whose roots are a third apart can be used as substitutes for each other, regardless of the presence or absence of a seventh. This is especially effective when the melody note belongs to both chords. When the harmony is diatonic, there are two common tones in the triads. For example, the ii chords can be substituted for the IV chords, and vice versa, iii or vi can be used in place of I. In cases where the harmony is more chromatic, a single tone may be common to both chords (and it may be the seventh of one of the chords, as in G7 and B♭m with F in the melody).

c. *Tritone-related chords.* Two dominant seventh chords (with or without extensions) whose roots are a tritone apart can be substitutes for each other. They will have two pitches in common, taking into account enharmonic spelling. Comparing a D7 chord (D–F♯–A–C) and an A♭7 chord (A♭–C–E♭–G♭), the roots are a tritone apart, and the third of one is the seventh of the other and vice versa. An example appears in measure 22, Ex. 15-2. The A♭7 takes the place of a continuation of the D7. The final cadence in the tune "Tenderly" is Fm7–E7–E♭7; the E7 is a substitute for the usual dominant seventh, B♭7.

2. Harmonic elaboration

a. *Embellishing chords.* Chords are often added before an essential chord, especially at cadences. For example, in C Major at a half cadence, instead of moving immediately to a G7, the performer or arranger may use a Dm7 that delays and embellishes it and adds harmonic motion. The final cadence is delayed and embellished in Ex. 15-2 by the chords in measure 31.

b. *Different harmonies for repetitions.* A melodic repetition is an invitation to vary the harmony through chord substitution and harmonic elaboration.

c. *Adding harmonic tension.* As in "classical music," the introduction of tension and release can enhance the harmonic effect. Chords of higher tension, such as the major seventh chord, can be used to give a measure of tension, which is then released by an added sixth chord that follows (Ex. 15-2, mm. 7–8, 15–16, 19–20, 23–24, 30, 31–32).

Example 15-6 Chord substitution and harmonic elaboration of a simple folk melody, "Au claire de la lune"
a. Simple version.

Example 15-6 (*continued*)

b. Jazz version

Moderate swing

As you compare the two versions in Ex. 15-6, you will notice that (b) has clef and meter signs only on the first system. This is a convention in jazz notation for scores and parts. The tempo marking "Moderate swing" indicates a tempo of about ♩ = 120. The "back beats," the second half of each beat, are delayed slightly (as if they occurred on the last eighth of a triplet) and are played with a slight accent. Several chord substitutions have been used (the second chord in bars 1 and 2, for example). Circle of Fifths progressions embellish the harmony (bars 3, 11–13, and 15). The repetition of the melody in bars 5–8 has been harmonized as in "the blues" (notice the melody is altered to give it a "blue note"). The "sting " chord is used in bars 8 and 9.

Chord voicing in the piano part gives the bass notes to the left hand and tightly voiced chords to the right hand arranged for smooth voice leading. A jazz instrumentalist (on alto saxophone, for example) could improvise on the tune or make variations based on the indicated harmonies ("the changes"). The A–A–B–A form of the folk song melody is identical to that of the standard popular song, except in miniature, each phrase being four bars in length. In the thirty-two-bar popular song, each phrase is eight bars long. The "B" section is called the *bridge*, which often modulates from the original key. The bridge in Ex. 15-6a) makes a short visit to C Major in bars 9–12.

Short Glossary of Jazz Terms

Ax. Jazz slang for any kind of instrument.

Back beats. The second half of each beat in simple meters. In a measure in common time consisting of eight eighth notes, the back beats occur on the even numbered eighths.

Big band. Large jazz ensemble, such as the dance bands of the swing era and the stage bands or jazz lab bands in a college setting.

Blue notes. Melodic pitches that are "bent" or altered in the manner of blues singing. This involves most often the third and seventh degrees of the major mode.

Break. Transition between choruses, often given to a soloist without accompaniment.

Bridge. The "B" section in a standard popular song whose structure is A-A-B-A.

Changes. The chord changes or set of harmonies in a given tune or arrangement.

Chart. The score of an original tune or an arrangement.

Chorus. The main section of a song, excluding the bridge and any verses. *See also* Jazz chorus.

Combo. Small jazz ensemble (two to about eight musicians).

Comping. Keyboard accompaniment to jazz improvisation.

Fake book. A large collection of standard songs and tunes, often presented in lead sheet notation.

Head. The written down or memorized ensemble passage, as opposed to the solo jazz choruses.

Head arrangement. An arrangement played by the band from memory. There may or may not be a written-out score and parts.

Jazz chorus. Improvised solo on the harmonies of a given song or the blues. In a jazz combo one of the performers may play several choruses.

Lead sheet. Melody with chord symbols, with or without the inclusion of lyrics.

Lead. The part or the performer that carries the most important melodic material. The lead may be the vocal part or the highest instrument part in a "soli" passage.

Lick. An improvisational jazz figure, often associated with a particular performer.

Riff. A short melodic idea that is continuously repeated over changing harmonies, often with slight alterations to accommodate the harmonies.

Scat. Solo vocal jazz improvisation involving nonsense syllables.

Soli. A group of like instruments, such as saxes or trombones, playing together in the foreground, characterized by close voicing and note-against-note rhythms.

Standard. A well-known song or tune that has become part of the jazz and popular music repertoire.

Tag. Coda or extension on the end of a tune.

Vamp. An introductory figure that can be repeated any number of times until all performers are ready to begin.

Walking bass. The bass part moves in steady quarter notes or eighth notes, mainly stepwise.

EXERCISES   **EXERCISE 15-1** The first six measures of Ex. 15-1 are given below with lead-sheet chord symbols showing the vertical sonorities on each beat of measure 1. Continue in the same manner for each beat of the remaining measures.

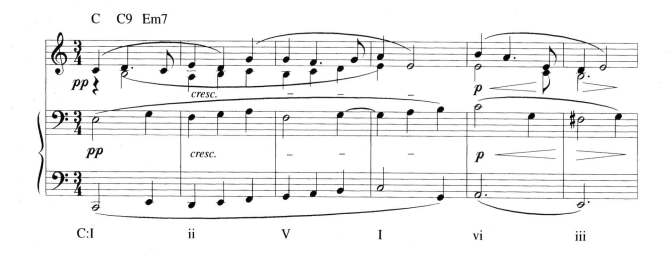

EXERCISE 15-2 The basic chord progression in Exercise 1 is given in roman numerals. Identify the decorative pitches (notes that are nonharmonic tones for the roman numeral chord analysis).

EXERCISE 15-3 Complete the harmonization of the given melody using the roman numerals as a guide.

EXERCISE 15-4 Make a piano arrangement of Ex. 15-2 using the beginning below. Vary the pattern in measures 17–24.

*EXERCISE 15-5 Complete the piano accompaniment for this arrangement for SSA choir of the folk song, "Ev'ry night when the sun goes in."

*EXERCISE 15-6 Write a jazz solo for trumpet or saxophone in concert pitch over the "changes."

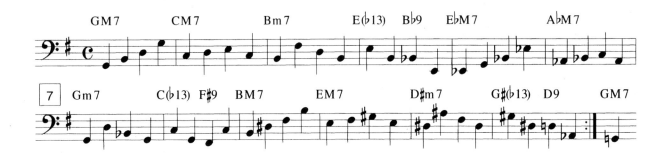

CHAPTER 16

CHROMATIC HARMONY

Example 16-1 Chorale from *Trois Chorals pour Grand Orgue,* No. 1 in E, by César Franck (1822–1890).

Example 16-1 (*continued*)

Example 16-1 (*continued*)

QUESTIONS FOR DISCUSSION

1. The organ chorale by Franck, Ex. 16-1, is in E, according to the composer. What other keys are established in the piece?

2. Some sections of the piece seem to focus on a definite tonality, but in others the tonality is in doubt. Where are these sections, and what devices are used by Franck to obscure the tonality?

3. What methods does Franck use to modulate to remote keys?

4. In Chapters 12 and 13 we discussed augmented sixth chords, third relations, borrowed chords, and irregular resolution. Can you find examples of each of these harmonic devices in Ex. 16-1?

5. *Chromatic harmony often leads to tonal ambiguity, which in extreme cases can lead to atonality. Is this a fair statement?*

6. In what sections in sonatas and symphonies of the eighteenth and nineteenth centuries is one most likely to find chromatic harmony?

DEFINITIONS, PRINCIPLES, AND OBSERVATIONS

As we have seen in Ex. 12-2 and Ex. 13-1, chromatic harmony in the form of third relation and altered chords had already appeared in the Renaissance and early Baroque eras. Bach was a master of chromatic harmony (as can be seen in the *Kyrie* and *Crucifixus* from his *Mass in B Minor*, *Fugue 4* from *WTC I*, and many other pieces). Mozart's fantasias (see Ex. 16-2) and Beethoven's quartets (see Ex. 14-1) are excellent examples of chromaticism in the Classic and early Romantic periods (review also Ex. 11-1). It is in the nineteenth century, however, that Chopin, Liszt, Wagner, Franck, and others developed the art of tonal chromaticism to a very high degree. The more chromatic a work becomes, the more ambiguous the tonality becomes. Composers who continued the trend eventually abandoned tonality altogether in our own century, as we shall see in later chapters. Techniques used in chromatic harmony are outlined below.

A. THE MODULATING SEQUENCE. Measure numbers in the following discussion refer to Ex. 16-1.

1. A modulating sequence consists of a musical idea with a self-contained harmonic progression or "harmonic module" that is repeated at a higher or lower pitch level. There may be one or more repetitions, but rarely more than three. The figure beginning in measure 5 is repeated twice, each time at a higher pitch level. The phrase beginning in measure 8 is sequenced down a step. Similar sequences begin in measures 19, 23, 28, and appear elsewhere throughout the remainder of the piece.

2. The interval between members of the sequence may be varied or fixed. The figure beginning in measure 5 is given a sequence up a step, then up a third. The sequence beginning in measure 19 descends by major third, with the third member moving up an octave before continuing the sequence.

3. Sequences may be tonal (diatonic) or real (chromatic, or exact transpositions). All of the sequences in Ex. 16-1 are real, with the exception of the one beginning in measure 5, where the first chord of each sequence member is a diatonic chord (I, ii, and IV); the second chord of each member, however, responds to real transposition (v, vi, and i).

4. Some small variations of melody, rhythm, or harmony often appear in the repetitions. In a three-member sequence, the third member is usually varied.

5. A longer sequence may exhibit fragmentation, where a smaller part of the original musical idea continues the sequence. An example of this occurs in the sequence beginning in measure 36. The two-measure musical idea is sequenced down a minor third, after which only the first measure of the idea continues the sequence, rising by half steps.

6. A chromatic sequence has the effect of obscuring the tonality so that a new tonality (or the resumption of the original tonality) may be established following the sequence.

Example 16-2 Phantasie, K. 475 by W. A. Mozart (1756–1791), measures 1–18.

B. DECEPTIVE PROGRESSIONS. Measure numbers in this discussion refer to Ex. 16-2.

1. Deceptive progressions include deceptive cadences, irregular resolutions of chords (especially dominant and diminished seventh chords), and unexpected modulations. Measure 2 sets up an expected resolution to the tonic, but measure 3 substitutes a diminished seventh chord. Measure 5 seems to contain a Neapolitan triad, but moves instead to its dominant, leaving us temporarily in D♭ Major. The diminished seventh chord in measure 8 sounds like a vii°7 in D♭ Major but resolves instead as a neighboring vii°7 to an E♭ minor triad, which in turn resolves to a B Major triad enharmonically, as if it had been a iii$_4^6$.

2. Each harmony may have different relationships with the chord that precedes it and the chord that follows it. The F♯ major-minor seventh chord in measure 11 has a dominant relationship with the B major chord that precedes it; the move to the A major-minor seventh chord in measure 12 is by third relation.

3. A chord may proceed to another chord that has no functional harmonic relationship with it but is connected by smooth voice leading. The G major-minor seventh chord in measure 14 moves to the E♭ minor triad in measure 15 by stepwise voice leading.

4. Modulation to a remote key can be accomplished by chromatic alteration. Measure 16 seems to be in the key of B Major. When the tonic is changed to B minor by lowering the third of the chord, G Major can be reached in measure 18 by third relation involving two common tones.

C. PROGRESSION BY CHROMATIC ALTERATION. Measure numbers in this discussion refer to Ex. 16-3.

1. The tonality is made increasingly ambiguous as chord members are altered in a progression, changing the chord qualities. In measure 2, the change in the left-hand chords from E to E♭ sounds like an appoggiatura resolving to a diminished seventh chord with dominant function. The subsequent move in measure 3 where F♮ replaces the F♯ negates that function. When the top note of the chord moves to D, a half diminished seventh chord results whose harmonic function is in doubt. We must wait until measure 4 for a relatively stable resolution to an E7 chord.

2. With only one or two chord members changing in the voice leading, the effect is of seamless chromatic motion. This is exemplified throughout the phrase from the beginning through the downbeat of measure 12.

3. Harmonic stability can be resumed at cadence points. A half cadence in E minor is achieved in measure 12, and the tonic key is reestablished with a return to the tonic chord in measure 13.

4. Harmonic stability can be further postponed by deceptive moves. A deceptive cadence from V^7 to vi occurs in measure 21. An even more deceptive move occurs in measure 23. The C dominant seventh chord comes as a very dramatic interruption of the expected cadence. It functions much like an inverted augmented sixth chord, finally resolving to the dominant on beat 3 of measure 24. The final authentic cadence serves to resolve all of the foregoing chromatic and deceptive progressions.

Example 16-3 Prelude, Op. 28 No. 4 by Frédérick Chopin (1810–1849).

EXERCISES   **EXERCISE 16-1** Continue the sequence; cadence in D minor.

EXERCISE 16-2 Copy out the bass line of Ex. 16-1, measures 47 to the end. Indicate each of the cadences by showing the key in effect, identifying the cadential chords with roman numerals, and naming the cadence type.

EXERCISE 16-3 Make a four-part realization of this figured bass. Make the top part as melodically convincing as you can.

EXERCISE 16-4 Compose a piano accompaniment for this violin melody.

***EXERCISE 16-5** The figured bass below can provide the harmony for a well-known standard popular song. Make a chordal realization with lead sheet chord symbols.

*EXERCISE 16-6 Make a roman numeral chord analysis of the realization you made for Exercise 16-5.

*EXERCISE 16-7 Using the realization you made for Exercise 16-5 as a starting point, make a piano arrangement with the melody of the popular song mentioned above. If you do not know the song, you may write a new melody to fit the harmonies.

*EXERCISE 16-8 Below is a partially completed setting of "Amen" based on the famous "B-A-C-H" motive (remember that in German music, B = B♭, and H = B♮). Complete the setting.

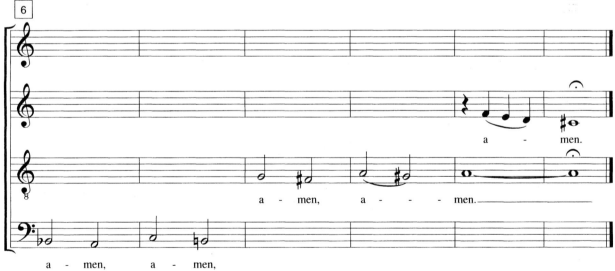

CHAPTER 17

THE MUSIC OF RAVEL
AND DEBUSSY

Example 17-1 Movement I from *Sonatine* by Maurice Ravel (1875–1937).

Example 17-1 (*continued*)

Example 17-1 (*continued*)

Example 17-1 (*continued*)

Example 17-1 (*continued*)

QUESTIONS FOR DISCUSSION

1. How would you describe the texture at the beginning of Ex. 17-1? Where is the melody? the harmony? How is the voice leading handled?

2. What is the tonic and the mode established in measures 1–5? What "scale" or "collection" is used in Ex. 5-1 p taken from "Voiles" by Debussy?

3. Ever since the late Renaissance, the strongest and most prevalent type of cadence is the authentic cadence. What kinds of cadences are used in Ex. 17-1?

4. What kinds of cadences do you find in Ex. 15-1, also by Ravel and in Ex. 7-1 by Debussy?

5. Dominant seventh and ninth chords are numerous in these examples. How are they resolved? How are they used in progressions?

6. A pentatonic pitch collection includes a major and a minor triad. What other sonorities can be made from a pentatonic pitch collection such as E-G-A-B-D? Locate some of these sonorities in Ex. 17-1 and in Ex. 7-1. What is the term commonly used for these sonorities?

7. Repetition and sequence play an important role in the continuity of phrases in the music of Ravel and Debussy. Describe their use in the examples we have been considering thus far.

8. There are many similarities of style in the music of Ravel and Debussy. What style traits do they share? In what ways do they differ?

9. How would you characterize the use of counterpoint by Ravel and Debussy?

10. We have seen in Chapter 16 how composers of the late Romantic era used chromatic harmony and pervasive modulation to create tonal ambiguity. What techniques does Debussy (and Ravel, to a lesser degree) use to create tonal ambiguity?

11. The term *impressionistic music* has been used to describe the style of Debussy, Ravel, Ibert, Delius, and others. What reasons can you give for the use of this term? Many musicians consider it an inappropriate term. Why?

DEFINITIONS, PRINCIPLES, AND OBSERVATIONS

Debussy and Ravel were the leaders in the creation of a new kind of music that sought to evoke a mood or impression through colorful harmony, unorthodox voice leading, and tonal ambiguity. Debussy's music has been associated with the impressionist paintings of the last twenty years of the nineteenth century, especially the work of Claude Monet. For this reason, French music at the turn of the century has been called "impressionistic music." Debussy's music has a more definite connection, however, with the poetry of Verlaine and Mallarmé and the Javanese music he heard at the World Exposition in Paris in 1889. Style characteristics of the music of Debussy and Ravel are examined in terms of harmonic, melodic, tonal, temporal, and textural usage.

A. SONORITIES

1. Triads of all types are used abundantly, often in a modal context. The augmented triad appears frequently in whole-tone passages.

Example 17-2 Augmented triads in the Prelude from *Pour le piano* by Debussy (measures 43–46).

2. All types of seventh chords are employed for the sake of harmonic coloration. The major-minor seventh chord is often used in contexts other than the dominant seventh (see Ex. 7-1, mm. 1–8).

3. Extended sonorities—ninth, eleventh, and thirteenth chords—are far more common in this style than in earlier styles and in German music of the same period.

Example 17-3 Extended chords in *Menuet sur le nom d'Haydn* by Ravel (measures 1–6).

4. Sonorities derived from the pentatonic collection—chords emphasizing perfect fifths and fourths, major seconds and minor sevenths—are frequently encountered (see Ex. 7-1, mm. 23–28).

5. Chords with added tones are common (see Ex. 7-1, mm. 35–41, Ex. 15-4 and Ex. 17-1, mm. 23–26).

6. Polychords begin to appear. Ravel's *Jeux d'eau*, for example, contains an extended passage that combines F♯ and C major triads.

B. HARMONIC PROGRESSION

1. The traditional resolution of dominant seventh chords and extended dominants is often avoided (see Ex. 17-1, mm. 6–13).

2. *Chord planing*—movement of all chord members in parallel—is a very common trait (see Ex. 15-1, mm 25–35, and most of Ex. 17-1).

3. Root movement by step and by third is more frequently used than in previous periods. Progressions involving third-related chords with no common tones are exploited for their exotic harmonic quality.

4. Modal progressions and cadences are more prevalent than traditional tonal progressions and cadences.

C. MELODY

1. Melody in Debussy and Ravel is frequently derived from modal, pentatonic, whole-tone, and gapped or exotic scalar resources. *Voiles*, from Preludes, Book I, uses whole-tone resources in the opening and closing sections and pentatonic resources in the middle section. Gapped scales figure in music with Spanish flavor, such as Debussy's *La soiré dans Granade* from *Estampes*.

Example 17-4 Lydian and Mixolydian modal combination in *L'isle joyeuse* by Debussy (measures 17–18).

2. Melodies often feature chord seventh, ninth, eleventh, added tones, or pitches unrelated to the harmony. The melody depends upon the accompanying harmony to provide the tonal context.

3. Melodic ideas are often developed by immediate repetition and subsequent fragmentation (see Ex. 17-1, mm. 6–12).

4. Melody may avoid the strong beats through use of suspensions, leading rests, or syncopations.

5. The melody may employ unusual doublings, such as in the outer voices (see Ex. 7-1, mm. 1–5).

D. TONALITY

1. The tonal focus may be clear or ambiguous depending on the scalar resources and the character of the harmony.

2. When the music is tonal, it is generally diatonic. Occasional degree inflection may occur (the first part of "Les entretiens de la belle et de la bête" from *Ma mère l'oye* by Ravel is a good example).

3. When the music is modal, the tonal center may shift or migrate, clearly established only at strong cadences (Ex. 7-1 exemplifies this).

4. Any tone in a pentatonic collection may be established as a tonic. Music that makes liberal use of pentatonic resources may shift the tonic among the available tones, or may establish a single tone as the tonic.

5. Tonal ambiguity is created through the use of the whole-tone collections, lack of strong cadences in modal music, quartal harmony, bitonality, and chord planing.

E. TEMPORAL CHARACTERISTICS

1. The metrical pulse may be strong and regular (Debussy: *Children's Corner Suite*, "Golliwogg's cake walk") or almost lacking (*Children's Corner Suite*, "Le petit berger").

2. Both Ravel and Debussy occasionally make use of asymmetric meters and changing meters.

3. Melody and accompaniment are set apart from each other by rhythmic means; the metrical pulse may be maintained by the accompaniment while the melody is free.

4. Triplets are a favorite rhythmic "diversion." Cross rhythms of two against three and three against four are not uncommon.

5. A favored device in triple meter is the hemiola.

F. TEXTURE

1. The most common texture is homophonic, with the melody on the top.

2. Formal polyphony is almost completely lacking; however, the "counterpoint" of foreground and background is usually maintained. Countermelody is occasionally encountered.

3. Melody doubled in the outer voices with harmony between is a new and often used texture. Colorful doublings such as two octaves above or doublings at other intervals are used occasionally.

4. Textures may be thin or thick; the number of tones sounding simultaneously often varies widely within a short space of time.

EXERCISES

EXERCISE 17-1 Choose a short piece by Debussy or Ravel, make a photocopy of it, and indicate with a colored marker examples of various style traits, identifying them by using the proper letters and numbers from the outline above.

EXERCISE 17-2 Complete the accompaniment in a similar style. Indicate harmonies as shown in measure 1.

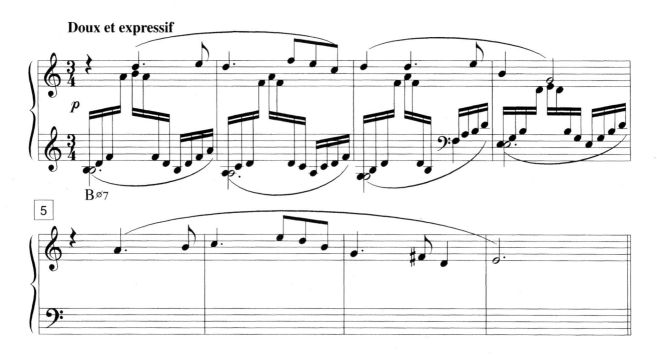

*EXERCISE 17-3 Write an accompaniment in the style of Debussy or Ravel for this bittersweet song. The setting is to be for soprano voice with harp or string quartet.

CHAPTER 18

TECHNIQUES BORROWED FROM THE MUSICS OF NON-WESTERN CULTURES

During the eighteenth and nineteenth centuries, composers in Europe and America often made use of folk music of their native lands. In the late nineteenth and throughout the twentieth century, composers have turned more and more to world music for techniques and textures to color their own music. This chapter will examine some of these. It must be stressed, however, that musics of various cultures outside of the Western tradition must be heard to be properly appreciated. Notated examples such as the following can show some techniques, but qualities such as vocal and instrumental timbres and tuning systems cannot be expressed adequately by our notation system.

Example 18-1 Rhythmic patterns in Gahu, West African percussion ensemble music. (Adapted from *Drum Gahu* by David Locke, © 1987, 1998 by White Cliffs Media Co., Sacramento, CA, used by permission.)

Example 18-1 (*continued*)

Example 18-1 (*continued*)

Example 18-2 Rag Bhairav; excerpt of a performance by Ram Narayan transcribed by Neil Sorrell. (Used by permission of the performer and transcriber.)

Example 18-2 (*continued*)

Example 18-2 (*continued*)

Example 18-3 Deninka, Bulgarian dance tune transcribed by the author.

Example 18-4 Typical ensemble passage in Javanese gamelan music. (Adapted from *"Javanese Gamelan Music"* by Mantle Hood, © 1967. Used by permission.)

Example 18-4 (*continued*)

QUESTIONS FOR DISCUSSION

1. How would you describe each of the examples in terms of (a) the temporal dimension, (b) the pitch dimension, (c) the color dimension, and (d) texture?

2. What characteristics do you find in each example that you would not expect to find in most Western music before the twentieth century?

3. Rhythm is obviously the central element in Ex. 18-1. Which parts have the least amount of variation in their patterns? Which have the most? How would you contrast the polyrhythmic effect with the rhythmic counterpoint in a Bach fugue?

4. Look at the signature of Ex. 18-2. What sort of scale does that produce? Is there any evidence of a tonal center in this music? What is the basic difference between the *alap* and *tal* parts of the excerpt? Are there any relationships between the melody of the *alap* and the melody of the *tal?*

5. Example 18-3 is a relatively fast dance. If you were conducting the instrumentalists, how would you show the beats? What pitch class appears to be DO in this music, and what is the prevailing scale? There are numerous ornaments indicated in the melody. What sort of added ornamentation would you suggest?

6. A gamelan is a special type of orchestra. In a large ensemble such as that shown in Ex. 18-4, all instruments share the meter. What else do they all share? How would you describe the texture? Why have the *saron, demung, kempjang,* and *ketuk* instruments been grouped together? What sets the *rebab* apart from all the others? What is the relationship between tessitura and rhythmic activity?

7. Repetition and improvisation play an essential role in all of the examples. Can you give examples of recent compositions by Western composers that make important use of these elements?

8. Taking a world view, what would you say are the unique contributions of Western music?

DEFINITIONS, PRINCIPLES, AND OBSERVATIONS

Twentieth-century composers have made use of various techniques that can be observed in the examples. The discussion that follows considers them in terms of the temporal dimension, pitch, color, and texture.

Techniques in the Temporal Dimension

A. POLYRHYTHM

1. Several parts with independent rhythmic patterns that share a metric frame may be combined to produce a polyrhythmic texture. In example 18-1, the *gonkongui,* similar to a cowbell, keeps a basic, unchanging pattern. Each of the drums has its own pattern that allows for some small variations, with the exception of the *kaganu,* whose pattern does not vary.

2. Some parts in an ensemble may be fixed, while others allow for improvisation. The lead drum part in Ex. 18-1 is totally improvised, drawing from a number of traditional rhythmic patterns. It allows for dynamic contrast and accentuation. Note in Ex. 18-4 that some instruments have fixed rhythmic patterns, while others allow for variation. The *rebab* part is improvised.

3. Rhythmic activity is often directly proportional to the tessitura of the instruments: higher (smaller) instruments tend to have greater rhythmic activity than lower (larger) instruments. The resulting texture is layered. This is especially true of the gamelan, and to a lesser degree the *gahu* ensemble.

4. In music with a strong metric pulse, cross-rhythms and cyclic rhythmic patterns may be used effectively. In Ex. 18-1 the lead drum often uses such devices (mm. 6–12 and 15–16). Although not shown in the examples, similar patterns are also common for the tabla in North Indian music. Three-note pitch patterns superimposed upon four-note rhythmic groupings are common in *gamelan* music, as shown in Ex. 18-5.

Example 18-5 Typical pitch cycles in gamelan music.

5. Rhythmic density may be used as a primary factor in the shaping of form. In the *tal* part of Ex. 18-2, important sections are delineated by changes in rhythmic density. In performance, rhythmic activity increases as the *tal* progresses.

B. PULSE AND METER

1. Music may be created that has no regular pulse, and therefore no meter is given. The *alap* section of a North Indian *raga* (or *rag*) performance is played by the soloist without a metrical pulse. A regular pulse is supplied by the tabla in the *tal* section (see Ex. 18-2).

2. When the pulses in a measure are not equal in length, an *asymmetric meter* results. The Bulgarian dance tune shown in Ex. 18-3 has three beats in the measure that are subdivided into a pattern of 3+2+2. Common metric subdivisions in Balkan music are 2+3 in $\frac{5}{8}$, 3+3+2, or 3+2+3 in $\frac{8}{8}$ meter, 2+2+2+3 or 2+3+2+2 in $\frac{9}{8}$ meter.

3. Different parts in an ensemble may have different meters. For example, *mariachi* music of Mexico often combines $\frac{3}{4}$ and $\frac{6}{8}$ rhythmic patterns in the guitar accompaniment parts.

Techniques in the Pitch Dimension

A. SCALE STRUCTURES

1. Gapped scales have more than a whole step between some consecutive scale degrees. When the pitch collection used in Ex. 18-2 is presented as a scale, the pitches are C, D♭, E, F, G, A♭, B. Gaps of an augmented second appear between $\hat{2}$ and $\hat{3}$ and between $\hat{6}$ and $\hat{7}$. The scale used in Ex. 18-3 is F, G♭, A, B♭, C, D♭, E♭. The augmented second is between $\hat{2}$ and $\hat{3}$.

2. Contemporary composers have experimented with non-Western scale structures such as the *slendro* and *pelog* tuning systems used in gamelan music. *Slendro* is a pentatonic collection that is roughly indicated by the scale sequence M2–M2–m3–M2–m3 (including the octave). The major seconds, however, are somewhat larger and minor thirds slightly smaller than their Western diatonic equivalents. *Pelog* is a pitch collection of seven pitches, five of which provide a background tuning that consists roughly of the scale se-

quence M3–m2–M3–m2–M2. The major thirds are somewhat smaller, and the major seconds slightly larger than Western diatonic equivalents. The excerpt shown in Ex. 18-4 uses the pelog tuning. The transcription can only approximate the actual pitches.

B. MELODY

1. Portamento and pitch bending are common features of the musics of many non-Western cultures. These techniques have become more and more a part of our own culture in the twentieth century. The flexibility of string and wind instruments and the human voice lends itself to these techniques. Relatively slow portamento between consecutive pitches has been indicated in Ex. 18-2. There is a great deal more subtle pitch bending not indicated in the notation, which must be heard in live or recorded performances.

2. Melody in many of the world's cultures is highly ornamented. Ornamentation tends to be highly stylized, drawn from traditional repertoires, rather than freely improvised. Western composers have experimented with liberal use of ornamentation in their works. In the *alap* section of Ex. 18-2, the *raga* is "unfolded" as each of its pitches is presented and ornamented until the full range has been exposed. In Balkan and Arab music, the melody is often presented by several instruments simultaneously, each adding its own embellishments. Bagpipe ornamentation, called *gaida*, of a simple Balkan tune is shown in Ex. 18-6.

Example 18-6 Typical ornamentation of a Balkan dance tune.

3. Presentation of a melody in several parts, each with its own fixed variation, produces a heterophonic effect. In the excerpt of gamelan music, the basic melody is played by the *saron* family. This melody is elaborated by traditional improvised figures on the *banangs, genders, rebab, tjelempung,* and *gambang.* The. melody is punctuated at specific points by the *kempjang, ketuk, kenong, kempul,* and *gong.* The *kendang* provides rhythmic accompaniment and signals changes in tempo and dynamics.

4. Ostinato patterns are frequently encountered in musics of non-Western cultures. Composers including Stravinsky, Bartók, Hovhannes, and Bloch brought ostinato techniques into the mainstream of twentieth-century music, and the minimalist composers have based their style upon ostinato and repetitive patterns.

Color and Texture

A. VOCAL AND INSTRUMENTAL COLOR

1. Western composers in the twentieth century have been fascinated by the variety of vocal color encountered in world musics and have incorporated some of those techniques into their own compositions.

   a. straight tone—complete lack of vibrato
   b. portamento, pitch bending, and microtonal alteration of scale degrees
   c. profuse ornamentation similar to that used by instruments

2. Western composers have written for non-Western instruments or combined them with standard orchestral instruments.

3. With expanding contact with percussion music such as that shown in Ex. 18-1 and the "emancipation of rhythm" that has taken place in the twentieth century, composers have produced an increasing amount of music for percussion. Percussion ensembles have become commonplace in music schools since about 1970, and a number of schools now have a regularly performing gamelan.

B. TEXTURE

1. Texture is of primary importance in many types of non-Western music. György Ligeti, Krzystof Pendercki, Yannis Xenakis, and others have shown that texture can be the major focus of a composition, rather than the exposition of themes and their development.

2. Music of the common practice period uses key scheme (and modulation) as a primary element in the delineation of form. In much of non-Western music, however, changes in texture more often delineate formal structure.

3. As we have seen in the examples and the discussion above, polyrhythmic and heterophonic textures are common elements in non-Western music.

4. Layered textures can be created by the superimposition of parts with different rhythmic activity; a positive relationship between tessitura and rhythmic activity is evident in several musical cultures, especially in Indonesian gamelan music.

C. UNIQUE TRAITS OF WESTERN MUSIC BEFORE THE TWENTIETH CENTURY

1. Imitative polyphony. With the exception of cultures that have been influenced by Western music, non-Western musics are almost completely lacking in imitative counterpoint.

2. Modulation and shift of tonal center. Most music outside of the Western tradition does not change key or tonal center. The use of drones, ostinato, and instruments with a limited number of available pitches tends to sustain a single tonal orientation.

3. Diatonic and chromatic harmony. Again, with the exception of those cultures that have synthesized some elements of Western culture, non-Western musics seldom display diatonic harmonic progressions and cadences. The Balkan dance tune, however, uses triads to harmonize the modal melody. The Balkan states and the Near Eastern countries have shown Western influences for centuries. The traditional musics of sub-Saharan Africa, India, China, Japan, and Indonesia exhibit fewer Western influences.

EXERCISES

EXERCISE 18-1 Continue the given patterns, allowing for slight variations in each part.

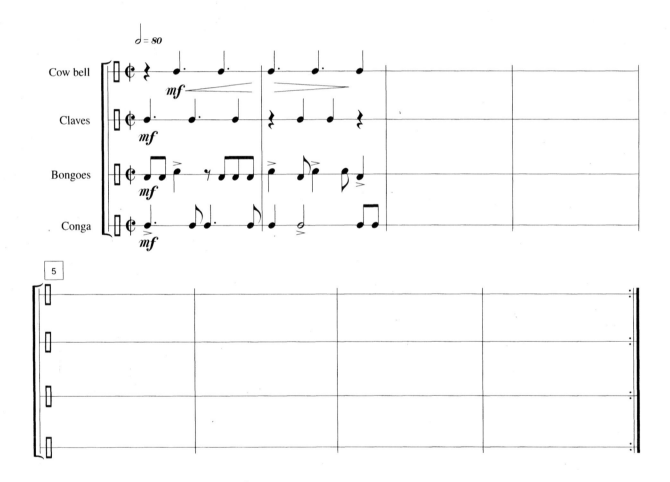

EXERCISE 18-2 Write a short piece for three hand-clappers. Devise a different pattern for each part. Perform your piece with other students in class.

EXERCISE 18-3 Using Ex. 18-2 as a point of departure, continue this melody for two or three more lines of notation. Try to avoid a feeling of meter. C is to be considered as the tonic.

EXERCISE 18-4 On one staff make a copy of the Hungarian folk song shown in Ex. 5-1f. On a second staff write an ornamented version of the melody for bagpipe.

EXERCISE 18-5 Provide a harmonization for this Balkan dance tune by writing chord symbols above the appropriate pitches. Note that the first part of the melody is in Dorian mode and the second part is in Mixolydian mode. The meter would be conducted in five beats with the third beat longer than the others.

EXERCISE 18-6 Continue the music below for another four to eight measures in imitation of a gamelan. Use only the pitches G, B, C, E, and F. The scoring is for two pianos, eight hands. As a class activity, let four students play a few of the completed exercises, extending them with improvisation in a similar style.

*EXERCISE 18-7 Complete the viola and cello parts for this short piece for string trio. Use only the octatonic pitch collection employed in the violin part.

EXERCISE 18-8 Several short recorded examples of non-Western musics will be played in class. Mark your responses on a copy of the form printed on the next page.

A FORM FOR STUDENT RESPONSES TO RECORDING OF NON-WESTERN MUSICS

As you listen to each example, put check marks in the appropriate boxes. After all examples have been played, be prepared to disucss them. They will be played again after the discussion.

	1	2	3	4	5	6	7	8
Tonality								
major/minor								
modal								
gapped scale								
modulate—key center changes								
Ornamentation								
little or none								
moderately ornamented								
highly ornamented								
Texture								
monody								
homophonic (accompanied melody)								
polyphony								
heterophony								
duo—melody and drums make counterpoint								
Meter								
non-metric								
duple or triple								
asymmetric								
meter shifts unpredictably								
Harmony								
chordal accompaniment								
drones								
Form								
song, strophic								
sectional with some sections repeated								
sectional, through-composed								
improvisatory								

Identify the source of each example.

Example 1 was _____

Example 2 was _____

Example 3 was _____

Example 4 was _____

Example 5 was _____

Example 6 was _____

Example 7 was _____

Example 8 was _____

CHAPTER 19

TECHNIQUES DEVELOPED
IN THE FIRST HALF OF THE
TWENTIETH CENTURY

Example 19-1 Ave Maria by Igor Stravinsky (1882–1971). (© Copyright 1934 by Hawkes & Son (London) Ltd. Copyright Renewed. Revised Edition © Copyright 1949 by Hawkes & Son (London) Ltd. Copyright Renewed. Reprinted by permission of Boosey & Hawkes, Inc.)

Example 19-1 (*continued*)

Example 19-2 No. 28 from *44 Violin Duets* ("*Sadness*") by Béla Bartók (1881–1945). (© Copyright 1933, 1939 for the USA by Boosey & Hawkes, Inc. Copyright Renewed. Reprinted by permission. © Copyright 1933 by Universal Edition. © Copyright renewed. All Rights Reserved. Used in the territory of the world excluding the United States by permission of European American Music Distributors Corporation, agent for Universal Edition)

Example 19-2 (*continued*)

Example 19-3 Interlude from *Ludus Tonalis* by Paul Hindemith (1895–1963). (© 1943 Schott & Co. Ltd., London, renewed. All Rights Reserved. Used by permission of European American Music Distributors Corporation, sole U.S. and Canadian agent for Schott & Co. Ltd., London.)

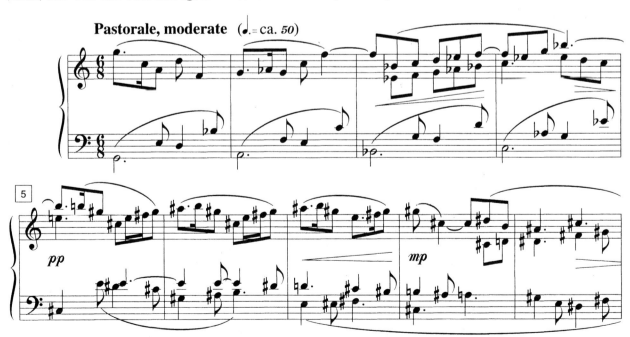

Example 19-3 (*continued*)

Example 19-4 No. 2 from *Goethe Lieder* by Luigi Dallapiccola (1904–1975). (© Edizioni Suvini Zerboni, Milan, used by permission.)

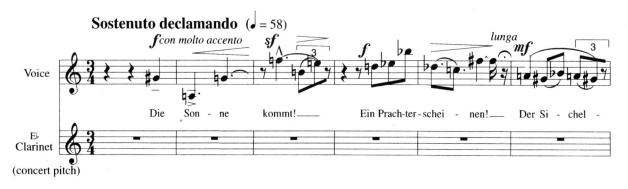

Example 19-4 (*continued*)

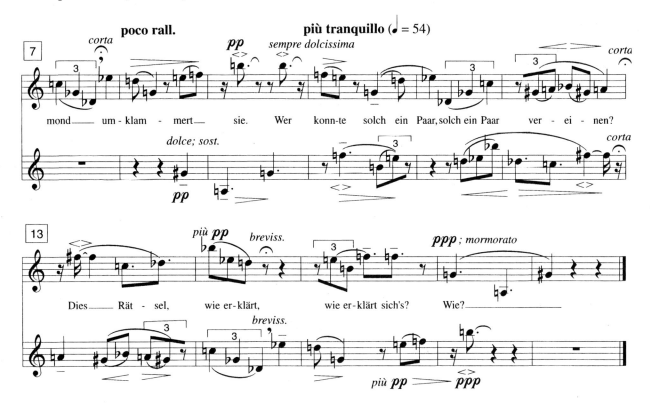

mond—— um - klam - mert—— sie. Wer konn-te solch ein Paar, solch ein Paar ver - ei - nen?

Dies—— Rät - sel, wie er - klärt, wie er - klärt sich's? Wie?——

The sun rises! A splendid brilliance! The crescent moon embraces
her. Who could such a pair unite? This riddle—how to solve it? How?

QUESTIONS FOR DISCUSSION

1. What is the tonal center in Stravinsky's *Ave Maria*, Ex. 19-1? What is unusual about the signature? the final chord?

2. Excluding the "amen," how would you describe the cadences in Ex. 19-1?

3. Ex. 19-1 is diatonic and triadic. What other kinds of sonorities do you find?

4. In the Bartók duo, what pitch seems to be DO? What leads you to that conclusion?

5. How does Bartók achieve the constant shifts in modal color? Can you associate a scale with the piece?

6. The tonal center at the beginning and end of Hindemith's *Interlude*, Ex. 19-3 is G. It shifts, however, several times in between. What is the tonal plan of the piece?

7. There are triads and seventh chords in Ex. 19-3, but many of the sonorities are not tertian. What intervals make up the sonorities in measures 8–12? How would you describe the chords at the climax in measures 15–17? What is the structural design of the piece?

8. The short song by Dallapiccola, Ex. 19-4, has no tonal center. What pitch collection is used for this piece? If you were to write an atonal piece, how would you keep it from suggesting tonality anywhere in the piece?

9. How is the clarinet part related to the voice part? How is the second half of the voice part related to the first half? What do these relationships have to do with the text of the song? How are the dynamics related to the text?

10. The opening phrase of the piece is five measures in length. How many different pitch classes are used in this phrase? The second phrase begins in measure 6 and continues to the word "sie" in measure 8. How many different pitch classes does this phrase contain?

11. Write down the series of pitch classes you found in the first phrase so that they are within a single octave. Underneath this, do the same for the series of pitch classes you found in the second phrase (omitting the repeated pitches A♮ and G♯). Do you see any relationship between the two sets of pitches?

DEFINITIONS, PRINCIPLES, AND OBSERVATIONS

The first half of the twentieth century saw the expanded use of chromaticism and modal harmony, which led to tonal ambiguity. While some composers continued to adhere to the major-minor tonal system, others developed new and expanded uses of tonality. Still others strove to create music without a tonal center.

Alternatives to the Major-Minor Tonal System

A. POLYTONALITY

1. Simultaneous use of two or more tonal centers. Each tonal center is associated with a key, mode, or independent pitch collection. Bitonality, or two competing tonalities, is most common.

2. The different tonalities may be assigned to distinct elements of the texture (melody, countermelody, harmony, accompaniment figures, and so on). Different signatures may be used if the bi- or polytonality is used consistently throughout the piece.

3. Some composers who have made extensive use of polytonality are Stravinsky, Bartók, Ives, and Milhaud.

4. The resulting harmony is often characterized by cross-relations and polychords.

Example 19-5 Bitonality: F Major and D Mixolydian.

B. DEGREE INFLECTION

1. Any degree of the scale or mode may be raised or lowered while the tonal center or tonic is retained.

2. Tones are inflected for the sake of color or to change the mode.

3. The mode or key may become ambiguous without losing the tonic.

4. "Blue notes" and intentional cross relations are two common uses of degree inflection.

5. Important tones in a melody may be strengthened when approached from below or from above by a half step requiring degree inflection.

6. Composers who have made extensive use of degree inflection are Hindemith, Ravel, Gershwin. and Bartók. In Ex. 19-2, the tonal center is A. All other scale degrees are treated to degree inflection, shifting the mode frequently throughout the piece. A and E are often approached by half step from below or from above. Note the striking cross-relation in measure 28.

C. PANDIATONICISM

1. Free use of the tones in a diatonic collection, not restricted by the principles of the traditional harmony.

2. Pandiatonicism is sometimes referred to as "the white-note technique."

3. Each part maintains its own melodic and harmonic orientation; if one part suggests the tonic harmony, another is likely to suggest the dominant harmony at the same time.

4. The composer most closely associated with this technique is Stravinsky. In Ex. 19-1 the pitch collection seems to be E Aeolian. All parts use the diatonic pitches freely. The prevailing tonal center, however, is C, with frequent cadences to E minor. Degree inflection appears in the use of F♯ and F♮.

5. In Ex. 19-6 all parts are limited to the pitches of the B♭ Major scale. Each part moves in a logical way, but the resulting sonorities do not produce functional triadic harmony.

Example 19-6 Pandiatonicism.

D. PITCH COLLECTIONS OTHER THAN MAJOR AND MINOR

    1. A renewed interest in modal melody and harmony is evident (see Chapter 17).

    2. Modes associated with folk music of Western and non-Western cultures are used frequently (see Chapter 18). Some composers experimented with tunings other than equal temperament.

    3. Freely constructed modes are encountered in the first half of the twentieth century. Some examples are:

        a. mixed modes, such as DO, RE, MI, FI, SO, LA, TE (incorporating the Lydian fourth degree and the Mixolydian seventh degree; see Ex. 5-1 o).

        b. gapped modes, such as DO, RA, MI, FI, SO, LE, TI.

        c. the octatonic or diminished scale (alternating whole and half steps; see Ex. 5-1 d).

        d. modes with more or fewer than seven pitch classes (the *Hirajoshi* scale, for example, is comprised of DO, RE, ME, SO, LE, sometimes referred to as the minor pentatonic scale).

    4. Experiments with *microtonal* music appeared before 1950, most commonly quarter tones. A quarter tone is half the size of a semitone. Use of microtones tones appeared in pieces by Ives, Bartók, Alois Hába, and Harry Partch.

E. QUARTAL HARMONY

    1. Sonorities that favor the perfect fourth, perfect fifth, minor seventh, and major second, as well as major and minor thirds and sixths—interval classes 2, 3, 4, and 5. The term *quintal harmony* is sometimes applied to music favoring sonorities based on the perfect fifth.

    2. Major and minor triads also are used freely in quartal harmony, but to a much smaller degree than in tertian harmony.

    3. Intervals of higher dissonance—minor second, major seventh, minor ninth, and tritone (interval classes 1 and 6)—are not part of pure quartal harmony; in works that feature quartal harmony they appear in places where a higher level of tension is required.

    4. Quartal sonorities can be derived from a pentatonic collection obtained by stacking up perfect fourths or fifths (for example: B–E–A–D–G or G–D–A–E–B yield a pentatonic collection of G–A–B–D–E; see Ex. 19-7).

Example 19-7 Some quartal sonorities that can be derived from pentatonic collection G–A–B–D–E.

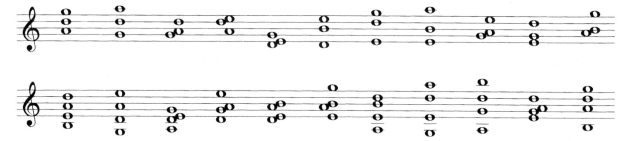

F. FREE ATONALITY

1. Musical continuity avoids melodic and harmonic construction that tends to establish a tonal center. Major and minor triads are generally avoided.

2. Free use of all twelve pitch classes predominates.

3. More than three consecutive pitches that can be associated with a diatonic scale are avoided.

4. The perfect octave is not used as a melodic or harmonic interval (except for orchestral doubling). Unisons may be used occasionally where two parts coincide momentarily.

5. Rhythm, dynamics, and texture are used to delineate form rather than tonal manipulation or "key scheme."

6. Melody tends to be disjunct and wide in range.

7. Schoenberg's music in the dozen years before his Op. 23 is most closely associated with free atonality.

G. TWELVE-TONE SERIALISM

1. The technique was developed by Arnold Schoenberg and first formally utilized in his Op. 23 No. 5, composed in 1923.

2. The principles of atonal composition continue to be applied (see Section F above).

3. The "technique of composition with the twelve tones," as Schoenberg called it, is governed by the following basic principles:

   a. Music is derived from a row or ordered set containing all twelve pitch classes of the chromatic collection.
   b. The row may be presented in four forms: Prime (forward), Retrograde (backward), Inversion (upside down), and Retrograde Inversion (backward and upside down).
   c. The pitch classes are deployed successively (melodically) or simultaneously (harmonically).
   d. No pitch class may be presented until all others have been sounded—with the following exceptions:

      i) a pitch may be repeated immediately
      ii) two or more pitches may be repeated as a subset, such as a trill, tremolo, or an obligato involving a segment of the row.

   e. Any form of the row may be presented in transposition. There are, therefore, forty-eight possible presentations of a row.

4. A matrix or "magic square" is a convenient way to show all forty-eight forms of a row. Ex. 19-8 shows the matrix for the song by Dallapiccola, Ex. 19-4. The prime sets are read from left to right, the retrograde sets are read from right to left, the inversion sets are read from top to bottom, and the retrograde inversion sets are read from bottom to top. The index numbers indicate the transpositions in total semitones above the original pitch class. P^0 is the prime set untransposed. I^0 is the inversion set untransposed. R^5 indicates the retrograde set that begins a perfect fourth above the untransposed

retrograde set (beginning on B♮, a P4 above F♯, the first pitch of R⁰). RI⁹ is the retrograde inversion set beginning a major sixth above RI⁰ (G♮ is a M6 above B♭).

Example 19-8 Twelve-tone matrix for Ex. 19-4.

I
↓

	0	1	11	9	3	8	6	7	2	5	4	10	
0	G♯	A♮	G♮	F♮	B♮	E♮	D♮	E♭	B♭	D♭	C♮	F♯	0
11	G♮	G♯	F♯	E♮	B♭	E♭	D♭	D♮	A♮	C♮	B♮	F♮	11
1	A♮	B♭	G♯	F♯	C♮	F♮	E♭	E♮	B♮	D♮	D♭	G♮	1
3	B♮	C♮	B♭	G♮	D♮	G♮	F♮	F♯	D♭	E♮	E♭	A♮	3
9	F♮	F♯	E♮	D♮	G♯	D♭	B♮	C♮	G♮	B♭	A♮	E♭	9
4	C♮	D♭	B♮	A♮	E♭	G♯	F♯	G♮	D♮	F♮	E♮	B♭	4
6	D♮	E♭	D♭	B♮	F♮	B♭	G♯	A♮	E♮	G♮	F♯	C♮	6
5	D♭	D♮	C♮	B♭	E♮	A♮	G♮	G♯	E♭	F♯	F♮	B♮	5
10	F♯	G♮	F♮	E♭	A♮	D♮	C♮	D♭	G♯	B♮	B♭	E♮	10
7	E♭	E♮	D♮	C♮	F♯	B♮	A♮	B♭	F♮	G♯	G♮	D♭	7
8	E♮	F♮	E♭	D♭	G♮	C♮	B♭	B♮	F♯	A♮	G♯	D♮	8
2	B♭	B♮	A♮	G♮	D♭	F♯	E♮	F♮	C♮	E♭	D♮	G♯	2
	0	1	11	9	3	8	6	7	2	5	4	10	

P → (left)   ← R (right)

↑
IR

New Techniques

A. IN THE PITCH DIMENSION

  1. *Polychords.* Two or more triads (or seventh chords) are sounded together. Ex. 19-9 shows several common configurations. Some examples are to be found in *Jeux d'eau* by Ravel, *Petrouchka* and *Le sacre du printemps* by Stravinsky, and *Sonata for two pianos and percussion* by Bartók.

Example 19-9 Polychords.

  2. *Tone clusters.* Sonorities consist of three or more tones spaced a whole or half step apart. Notable examples may be found in the piano music of Henry Cowell. Ex. 19-10 shows several ways of notating clusters.

Example 19-10 Tone clusters.

a) block chord, all pitches notated
b) highest and lowest tones notated; ♮ indicates white keys, ♭ indicates black keys
c) broken chord indicated with measured rhythm
d) broken chord indicated with grace notes

    3. *The major-minor sonority.* Chord members include root, fifth, major third and minor third. The most common configuration has the minor third on the top and the major third on the bottom. The reverse, however, is encountered as well. A configuration with the major and minor thirds adjacent to each other is used occasionally. Ex. 19-11 shows several voicings of this sonority.

Example 19-11 The major-minor sonority shown in various voicings.

    4. *Octave displacement.* Pitches of a melody (or tone row) may be altered by presentation up or down one or more octaves. Single pitches may simply be moved an octave up or down, or they may be doubled or sustained, as in Ex. 19-12.

Example 19-12 Folk melody, "The Ash Grove" altered by octave displacement.

B. IN THE TEMPORAL DIMENSION

1. *Unconventional metric schemes.* Asymmetric meter such as $\frac{5}{4}$, $\frac{7}{8}$, and $\frac{3+2+3}{8}$; music with frequently changing meter; and music with no meter (*senza mesura*) are encountered more frequently.

2. *Polyrhythms and polymetric music*

   a. Parts with independent rhythmic motives may be combined to create polyrhythmic textures like those we examined in Chapter 18.
   b. Parts in different meters may be combined.
   c. Parts with rhythmic patterns that go against the prevailing meter may be combined with parts that agree with the meter, resulting in cross-rhythms.

Example 19-13 Polymetric music.

a) Measure length is constant.   b) Implied meters are shown by beaming and phrasing.

3. *Displaced accents.* Striking rhythmic effects can be achieved by giving accents to notes that fall outside of the metric pulses. In Ex. 19-14 a rest appears on some of the strong beats, shifting the accent by a sixteenth note. In the third measure a cross-rhythm is created by accented three-note groupings.

Example 19-14 Displaced accents.

C. OTHER TECHNIQUES

1. *Klangfarbenmelodie.* A kind of melody that is shaped by changing tone color or timbre. The term first appears in Schoenberg's *Harmonielehre*, 1911. With this technique the notes of a melody are passed from instrument to instrument. The effect is often hightened by changes in dynamics, articulation, or instrumental doublings.

2. *Pointillism.* The term is borrowed from the painting technique to describe a musical texture in which notes are isolated from one another by rhythmic spaces (rests of various lengths), tessitura (octave displacement), or timbre.

3. *Simulaneity.* A texture resulting from the combination of two or more unrelated musical ideas. Charles Ives explored this texture early in the twentieth century. An extreme example appears in his Fourth Symphony, 1909–1916.

EXERCISES

EXERCISE 19-1 Continue the left-hand part in C Major.

EXERCISE 19-2 Write three variations on this folk melody setting. In the first, use some degree inflection in both parts. In the second, add some decorative pitches to the melody and apply some octave displacement. In the third, write a new bass line using the technique of pandiatonicism.

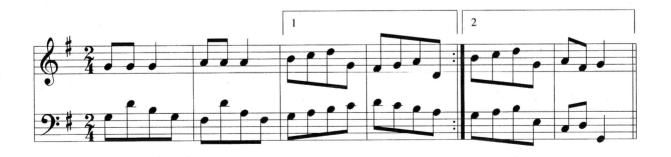

EXERCISE 19-3 Complete this short march-style piece for brass quartet using quartal harmony. The score is a two-staff reduction in concert pitch.

EXERCISE 19-4 Write a ten- to twelve-measure duet for two violins that uses one of the scales given below. You may use a few double-stops if you wish.

EXERCISE 19-5 The twelve-tone row given below was used by Webern in his *Symphony*, Op. 21. Complete the matrix using numbers to represent the pitch classes, then answer the questions that follow.

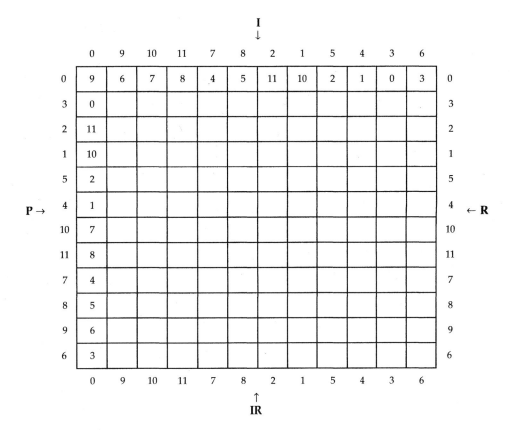

a. How is the first half of the row (hexachord 1) related to the second half (hexachord 2)?

b. What interval classes are contained in this row? (Remember that the interval class is the size of an interval in semitones and its inversion. Interval class 4, for example is a M3 or m6)

c. Which forms of the row are duplicates of other forms? How many distinct forms of this row are there?

*EXERCISE 19-6 Write a setting of the folk melody of Exercise 19-2 for woodwind quintet using the techniques of Klangfarbenmelodie, pointillism, octave displacement, degree inflection, and changing meters.

*EXERCISE 19-7 Compose a short piece, about twenty to twenty-four bars, for string trio in strict twelve-tone technique using the row given in Exercise 19-5.

CHAPTER 20

TECHNIQUES DEVELOPED IN THE SECOND HALF OF THE TWENTIETH CENTURY

Example 20-1 *Miserere* for six-part voices or mixed chorus by the author.

Pitch materials in this composition are based on a three-note cell consisting of a tone and a semitone. Four forms are used:

    a. ascending semitone followed by descending tone
    b. ascending tone followed by descending semitone
    c. descending tone followed by ascending semitone
    d. descending semitone followed by ascending tone

No clefs are given for any of the six parts; pitches are not specified, except as to register. Staff lines indicate high, middle, and low registers. Melodic intervals, however, should be carefully tuned.

Each part may be performed by one or more singers. When more than one are assigned to a part, an effort should be made NOT to match pitches.

Voices should be assigned such that the higher voices sing parts 1, 2, and 3 and the lower voices sing parts 4, 5, and 6. An optimum assignment would be S-S-A-T-B-B.

Example 20-1 (*continued*)

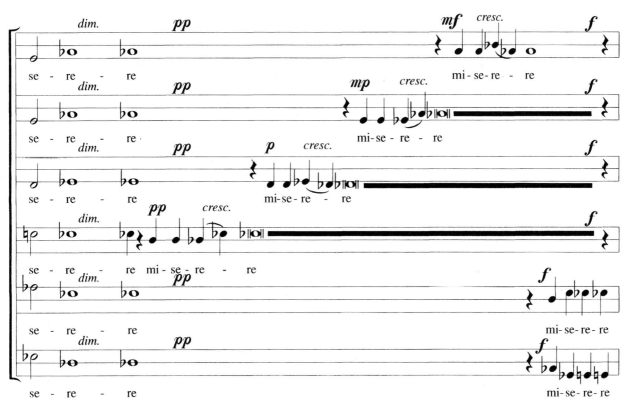

Example 20-1 (*continued*)

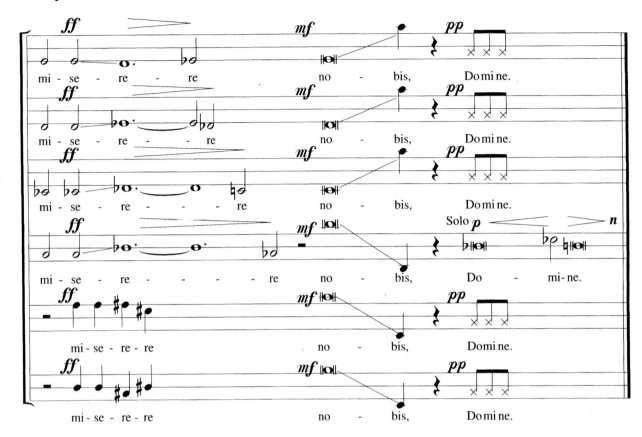

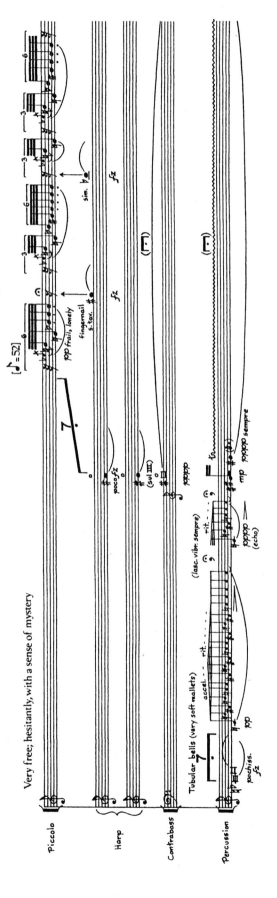

Example 20-2 No. 2 from *Madrigals, Bk. IV* (1971) by George Crumb (b. 1929). (© 1971 by C. F. Peters Corporation, used by permission.)

II. Tu cuerpo, con la sombra violeta de mis manos, era un arcángel de frío

[Through my hands' violet shadow, your body was an archangel, cold]

Example 20-2 (*continued*)

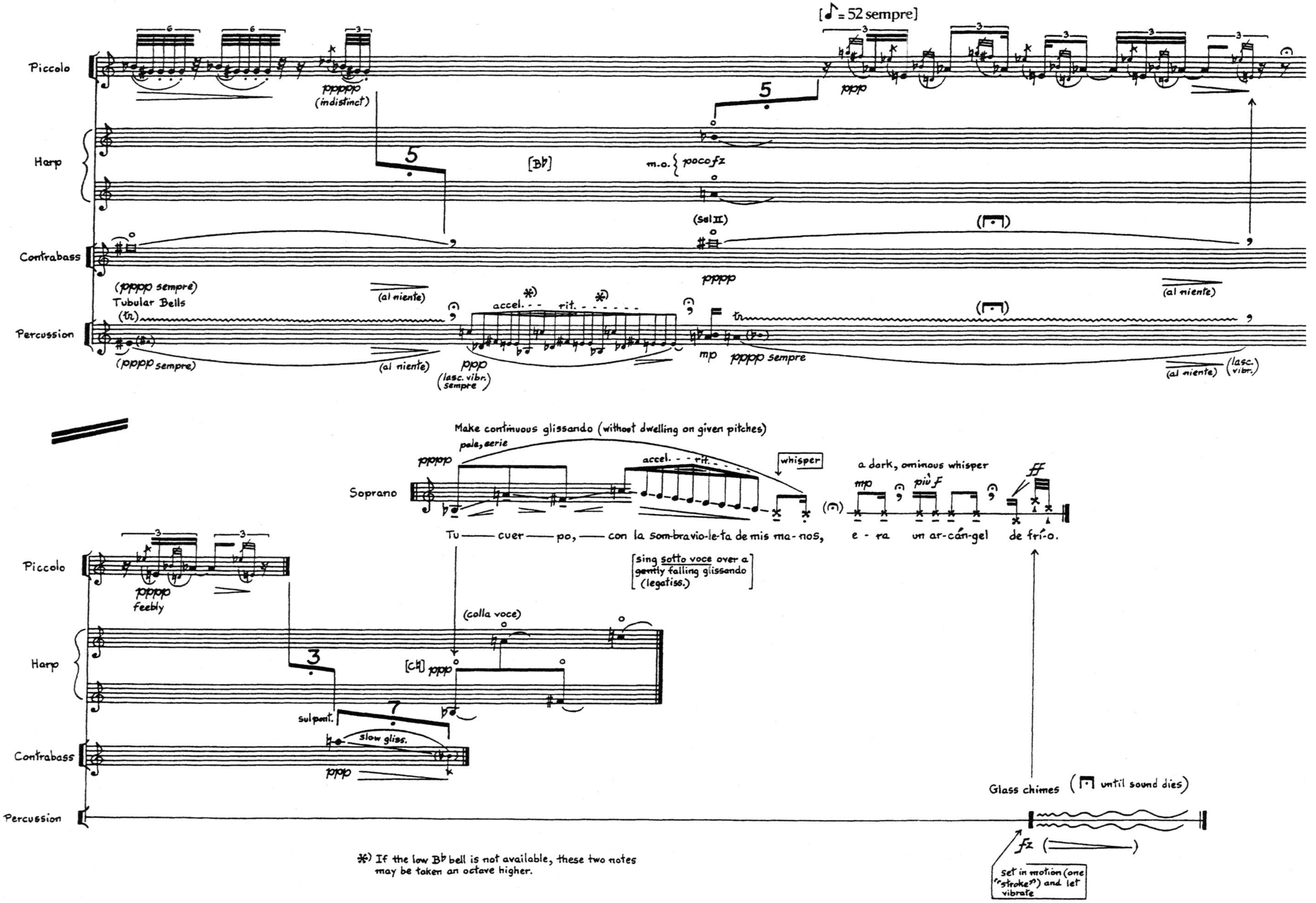

*) If the low B♭ bell is not available, these two notes may be taken an octave higher.

Example 20-3 No. 2: "La Source de Vie" from *Libre du Saint Sacrement* by Olivier Messiaen (1908–1992). (Reproduced by kind permission of Alphonse Leduc & Cie, Paris, France, sole publishers of the work for the entire world.)

*) The pedal part sounds an octave higher throughout

Example 20-3 (*continued*)

Example 20-4 Final section from *Magnificat* by Arvo Pärt (b. 1935). (© 1989 by Universal Edition A. G., Wien. All Rights Reserved. Used by permission of European American Music Distributors Corporation, sole U.S. and Canadian agent for Universal Edition A. G., Wien.)

Example 20-4 (*continued*)

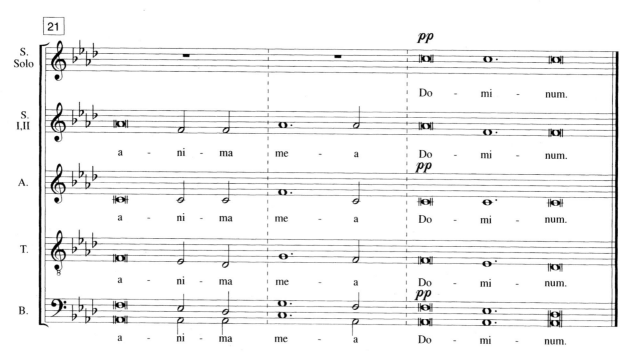

QUESTIONS FOR DISCUSSION

1. With the exception of Ex. 20-4, what elements of serial technique and notation practices can you detect in Exx. 20-1, 20-2, and 20-3?

2. What elements in each of the four examples are (a) specified by the composer, (b) left to the performers' choice, and (c) left to chance?

3. How would you describe the texture of each example?

4. What contrapuntal devices are used in the *Miserere*, Ex. 20-1?

5. Why has a three-line staff been used in the *Miserere*? How can you tell the whole steps from the half steps? How can the performers keep time without bar lines? Why have rests been used in some places but not in others when voices are silent?

6. How are the motives developed in the *Madrigal* by George Crumb, Ex. 20-2?

7. Discuss unusual features of the notation in Ex. 20-2. What is meant by the bracket and number between the first notes in the harp and the piccolo parts? Why do most of the notes in the harp part have note heads without stems?

8. How is the element of harmony related to register in the *Madrigal*?

9. Other than register and rhythm, what distinguishes the melody from the accompaniment in Ex. 20-3? How is the melody related to the accompanying chords? How many different sonorities are there in measures 1–7? Where else in the piece do you find these chords?

10. What is significant of the pitches in the pedal part in the Messiaen?

11. The excerpt from Arvo Pärt's *Magnificat*, Ex. 20-4, is representative of the musical style of the whole work, and it is typical of much of the composer's later works. How would you describe the tonality? What is the significance of the signature?

12. The use of sonority is certainly one of the most important features of Pärt's work. Discuss how the sonorities affect harmonic tension. How would you describe the cadences? Can you explain the unusual cadence at the end?

13. Discuss how texture, dynamics, and choral scoring delineate the formal structure.

14. Why are there no meter signatures in any of the examples? Examples 20-1 and 20-2 use no bar lines, Ex. 20-3 uses solid bar lines, and Ex. 20-4 uses both dashed bar lines and double bars. What reasons can you give for these differences? Discuss the feeling (or lack) of pulse in each of the examples.

DEFINITIONS, PRINCIPLES, AND OBSERVATIONS

Techniques developed in the first half of the twentieth century continued to be used and developed as the century progressed. The question of control became an important issue during the 1960s and early 1970s. On one hand, some composers demanded more and more control over all aspects of a composition, while on the other, composers wished to give performers—and the element of chance—a larger role in the creative process. In the late 1970s a number of important composers turned to the principles of romanticism for their inspiration. Since then a "neoromaticism" has grown ever stronger. A series of concerts and broadcasts by the New York Philharmonic produced in the late 1980s, called "The New Romaticism," was a showcase for the latest trends in concert music. At the end of the century, a lively variety of styles coexist. Major trends are briefly described below.

A. DEVELOPMENTS IN SERIAL TECHNIQUE

1. Serial techniques may be applied to dynamics, rhythms, articulations, and other elements. This technique is commonly referred to as *total serialism.* Examples may be found in the music of Anton Webern, Olivier Messiaen, Pierre Boulez, and Milton Babbitt.

2. Some composers apply serial technique freely, allowing for the use of triads and other structures that tend toward a tonal focus.

3. Some composers use a row to generate basic melodic and harmonic ideas for a piece, then compose without further serial constraints.

B. VARIETY IN THE DEGREE OF CONTROL BY COMPOSER AND PERFORMERS. The listing below describes music in order of diminishing control by the composer, increasing control by the performers, and, finally, control by chance procedures.

1. *Absolute control.* The composer retains complete control over all aspects of composition and performance. Examples: electronic or computer music designed and executed by the composer; music created and performed only by the composer.

2. *Allowance for interpretation.* Some scores indicate musical elements (pitch, duration, tempo, dynamics, articulation, phrasing, and so on) meticulously, but depend upon performers' skills for faithful execution of the music. Other scores leave some details to the interpretation of the performers.

3. *Controlled chance.* Some aspects of a composition are left to the choice of the performers. Examples: the number of repetitions of a figure or segment; a given sample marked "continue in the same manner ad lib."; rhythmic figures notated without note heads, showing only generalized pitch.

4. *Improvisation.* Aspects of a piece are invented on the spot (improvised) by one or more of the performers with or without musical guidelines provided by the composer, such as a given set of harmonies, or a melody for improvised variations.

5. *Indeterminacy.* Some aspects of the music are left to chance or to free choice by the performers. Examples: the performer or conductor chooses the order of movements or sections of the music; the performers freely interpret a score that is a graphic image.

6. *Aleatory.* Aspects of a piece are controlled by chance, such as the throw of dice (*alea* = dice), a shuffled deck of cards, or a random number generator.

C. ELECTRONIC AND COMPUTER-GENERATED MUSIC

1. *Musique concrète.* Actual ("live") sounds are recorded, then processed by various means including tape speed changes, tape reversal, tape editing, electronic filtering, ring modulation, mixing, and assembled into a composition available for performance on tape or compact disk. Example: *Gesang der Jünglinge* by Karlheinz Stockhausen (1956).

2. *Electronic synthesis.* Use of synthesizers for the generation of sounds that may be altered by tape editing, sequencing, and modulated by filters and other electronic modulation devices, assembled into a composition for performance on tape or compact disk. Example: *Silver Apples of the Moon* by Morton Subotnick (1967).

3. *Live performance plus electronic music.* The composer presents a score that includes the music for one or more performers and a graphic representation of a pre-recorded tape. In performance the performer(s) are responsible for proper synchronism with the taped music. Example: the *Synchronisms* series by Mario Davidovsky (1963–1974).

4. *Computer-generated music.* Computers can be programmed to produce music in a number of ways:

   a. Programmed digital data processed by a computer can be converted to electronic signals that, through an amplifier and speakers, produces the sounds of a composition. Originally depending on tedious punch card input to mainframe computers, this technique now uses sophisticated programs that can be run on personal computers.
   b. Computers can be used to process live or recorded sounds converted to digital data, then reconverted to electronic signals. This technique is similar to *musique concrète*, except that computers are substituted for tape recorders.
   c. Using the MIDI digital language, a "sequence" of events can be stored that will control a synthesizer, which in turn produces the sounds of a composition. Computer notation programs can be used in the creation of a composition, then, using the program's playback capabilities, can be recorded.
   d. A computer can "compose" music, given enough information (in the form of programmed algorhythms) for choices of pitch, rhythm, articulation, tempo, dynamics, structure, and so on.

D. INFUSION OF JAZZ, POP, FOLK, AND NON-WESTERN MUSICS

1. Some composers incorporate jazz figures in their compositions. The term *third stream* is often applied to this music. Leonard Bernstein's *Mass* (1971) is an example.

2. Many composers use techniques borrowed from non-Western musical cultures. Notable examples may be found in the music of Lou Harrison, Alan Hovhannes, and La Monte Young.

3. Some composers use a fusion of musical styles that incorporate contemporary techniques and various aspects of jazz, folk, and pop styles. Frederick Rzewski's variation set *The People United* (1978) is a good example.

E. TEXTURE AND TIMBRE

1. Composers including Georgy Ligeti and Krzysztof Penderecki produced music that promotes texture and tone color above melodic and rhythmic ideas.

2. Experimentation with extended techniques for instruments and voices adds greatly to the palette of timbres available to composers. Some of these are:

   a. multiphonics and harmonics on wind instruments, key clicks, humming or speaking through the instruments,
   b. unusual string sounds made by playing on or behind the bridge or percussive effects made with the bow or by knocking on the instrument,
   c. percussion effects, such as pitch bending and playing with a bass bow on mallet instruments, submerging a vibrating gong into a tub of water, ringing wine goblets, preparing the strings of a piano with various objects,

   d. harp sounds produced by bowing on the strings with a rosined length of twine and pitch bending using a glass rod on the strings,
   e. extended vocal techniques, whispering, half-voiced sounds, long glissandos, throat singing, extremes of range, vocalise, and nonsense syllables,
   f. newly created instruments, such as the array of percussion instruments created by Harry Partch, synthesizers, amplification and modulation of acoustic instruments and voices.
   g. use of folk and ethnic instruments.

F. MINIMALIST MUSIC

   1. The terms *minimalism* and *pattern music* denote music that is constructed from a limited range of musical materials.

   2. The texture consists of repeated rhythmic patterns and static harmony. Changes are gradual and take place over long time spans.

   3. Minimalist music is often strongly tonal. The harmony often features the rich sonorities of extended dominants and polychords.

   4. *Phase music* is a special type of minimalism in which a repeated pattern is presented at two slightly different speeds so that elements of the pattern slowly move in and out of phase. An early example is *Piano Phase* (1967) by Steve Reich.

   5. Other composers associated with minimalist techniques are Terry Riley, whose work *In C* (1964) uses aleatoric procedures; Philip Glass, best known for his theatrical work, *Einstein on the Beach* (1976); and John Adams, who uses rich harmonic textures and motoric rhythms in his works *Shaker Loops* (1978), *Harmonium* (1981), and the opera *Nixon in China* (1987).

   6. Late works by these composers are richer in vocal and instrumental color and allow for textural change to occur in shorter time spans. *Desert Music* (1983) by Steve Reich is an example of this.

G. "THE NEW ROMANTICISM"

   1. Two works that signal a trend toward a new romanticism are *Sinfonia*, for voices and orchestra, by Luciano Berio (1969), which incorporates quotations from Mahler and Ravel, and George Rochberg's String Quartet No. 3 (1976), which includes original music in the styles of Beethoven and Mahler.

   2. The trend seems to be a reaction against the extreme complexity and cerebral nature of post-Webern serialism and the excesses of avant-garde music of the late 1960s and early 1970s. Several composers associated with these older styles have become the leaders of the newer movement.

   3. Some general features are a reassertion of romantic values, including a balance of emotion and reason, a heightened interest in sound texture and color, and a conscious effort of composers to reach a wider audience.

   4. Some technical features are a fusion of styles (including jazz, folk, pop, and non-Western musics), a renewed interest in tonality, lyricism, and harmony, and use of advanced technology.

   5. The movement embraces a wide variety of "musical languages" from the complex and colorful orchestral works of Joseph Schwantner to the uncompromisingly Mahleresque "Alice in Wonderland" pieces by David Del Tredici.

EXERCISES

EXERCISE 20-1 Choose four telephone numbers at random from your telephone book. Let the numbers represent degrees of the major scale. Select the two that seem to make the best melodic phrases, choose a key, a meter, and assign rhythms, then notate the melody. Below is a sample.

3   5   8   3   4   4   2   3   4   5   1   8   9   0

Write a short paragraph explaining what part of the process is aleatoric, what part was chosen for you, and what part was your choice as composer.

EXERCISE 20-2 The binary number system is the native tongue of computers. Digits are represented solely by ones and zeros. The numbers 0 through 9 are represented as follows: 0 = 0000, 1 = 0001, 2 = 0010, 3 = 0011, 4 = 0100, 5 = 0101, 6 = 0110, 7 = 0111, 8 = 1000, 9 = 1001. In the duet for two handclappers below, the rhythm of the first part has been generated from the telephone number, 358-3442, used in the example in Exercise 20-1. The numbers were first expressed in the binary system, and then the ones were converted to quarter notes, and the zeros were converted to eighth notes. Notice that some of the quarters must be given as eighths tied over the bar line. Create the second handclapper's part in the same manner using another telephone number chosen at random.

EXERCISE 20-3 Rewrite the duet of Exercise 20-2 in $\frac{6}{8}$ meter. Perform this and the other version with another student.

EXERCISE 20-4 Below is the beginning of a piano piece in minimalist style. Continue the piece for another eight to twelve measures, introducing gradually small changes such as added notes, changes of pitch, or changes of rhythm as the piece progresses.

*EXERCISE 20-5 Construct an eight-measure piece for violin and cello based on the given six-element serial pitch row, rhythm row, and articulation row that follows the given plan. HINT: The result may be constructed as a palindrome.

Pitch row	E♮	C♮	B♭	F♯	C♯	G♮
Rhythm row	♩.	♪	♪	♪.	♩	♩. 𝄾
Articulations	>	.	'	–	slur	nothing

Structural Plan

	Measures 1–2	3–4	5–6	7–8
Violin	Pitch row: P⁰	I¹	RI¹	R⁰
	Rhythm row: P	R	P	R
	Articulations: P	R	P	R
Cello	Pitch row: I¹	P⁰	R⁰	RI¹
	Rhythm row: R	P	R	P
	Articulations: R	P	R	P
Dynamics	*p cresc. f*	*ff dim. pp*	*pp cresc. ff*	*f dim. p*

*EXERCISE 20-6 Compose a brief setting for unison speaking chorus, vibraphone, marimba, and temple blocks (set of five) of the following text:

The sun knows not how to tell the time.

Suggestions: assign different pitch collections and registers to the different parts. Indicate rhythms and generalized pitches for the chorus. Experiment with coloristic instrumental and/or choral devices. Use Exercise 20-2 as a model for texture and score layout.

*EXERCISE 20-7 Design a piece that combines performers' choice and elements of aleatory. Write down performers' instructions clearly, anticipating any possible questions they might have. Suggestions: explain how the piece is to start, continue, and end, what instruments or voices may be needed, and how any unusual symbols in the score are to be interpreted.

STYLE PROFILES

In Chapter 1, we defined the word *style* as "characteristics that define period, genre, region, an individual or group of composers, or manner of performance." In the Style Profiles on the pages to follow, we will define each of five periods or eras of music in terms of the four dimensions of music:

> Temporal dimension: meter and pulse, rhythm
>
> Pitch dimension: melody, harmony, tonality
>
> Structural dimension: texture, major genres, structural devices
>
> Color dimension: dynamics and articulation, scoring and instrumentation

Profiles are given for the Middle Ages, the Renaissance, the Baroque era, the Classical era, and the Romantic era. Because of the great variety in the styles of the twentieth century, individual stylistic traits and techniques have been discussed in chapters 17 through 20.

In order to summarize characteristics of style for any period, it is necessary to make generalizations and to ignore some details and exceptions. An effort has been made to avoid overly positive statements. The information is presented as a way to characterize each period in technical terms, rather than historical, social, or philosophical terms. Each profile presents the information in the same order so that comparisons can be made from one period to another.

Since space is limited, some important characteristics may have been omitted or given inadequate explanation. You and your instructor are encouraged to amplify these profiles through your own experience and class discussion. We hope that what is presented here will help you to gain a stylistic perspective as you continue your studies of music theory.

STYLE PROFILE: MIDDLE AGES

Temporal Dimension

METER AND PULSE

1. A system of *mensural notation* governs meter. The time signature governs the relationship between levels of note values. The beats (*tactus*) are grouped or subdivided in threes ("perfect") or twos ("imperfect"). Measure bars are not used until the seventeenth century. If the beats are grouped in threes and subdivided in twos, the meter in a modern transcription would be $\frac{6}{8}$.

2. Meters most often encountered are $\frac{3}{4}$, $\frac{6}{8}$, and $\frac{9}{8}$ in modern transcriptions.

3. The feeling of pulse is quite strong in all medieval music, with the exception of unaccompanied chant.

RHYTHM

1. Rhythm in the music of the twelfth and thirteenth centuries is governed by patterns called *rhythmic modes*. Using L = long and S = short, they are: LS, SL, LSL, SLL, LL, and SSS. In modern notation, the L is a quarter or dotted quarter, and the S is an eighth.

2. More rhythmic variety is evident in fourteenth- and fifteenth-century music, especially secular songs and dances.

3. Cadences are marked by longer notes in all parts.

4. Higher parts tend to move in shorter time values then lower parts.

5. A rhythmic device, called *hocket*, is a special feature, in which one part has short notes on the beat while another has short notes off the beat, creating a quick alternation of notes. In modern transcription the parts are written with eighth notes and rests.

Pitch Dimension

MELODY

1. Predominantly stepwise; leaps are rarely larger than a fifth; leaps of a tritone, major or minor seventh, major or minor ninth, and all augmented or diminished intervals are discouraged.

2. Melodic range rarely exceeds an octave.

3. Primarily diatonic; degree inflection is ruled by the principles of *musica ficta* (raising of the leading tone to the tonic and dominant at cadences, lowering B to B♭ to avoid the tritone).

4. After larger leaps the melody usually proceeds by step in the opposite direction. A notable exception, however, is a rising fifth followed by a rising half step.

5. Common dissonant figures: passing tone, neighbor tone, double-neighbor; accented passing or neighbor tones and appoggiaturas are used occasionally.

6. Long, melismatic phrases are used in the organa of Leonin and Perotin and the fourteenth-century madrigal and ballata; more syllabic melodies are used in the conductus and the secular motets.

7. Repetition, sequence, and periodic structures are common features, especially in secular vocal music and instrumental dances.

HARMONY

1. Consonance/Dissonance ratio is generally 3 to 1. The perfect fourth is not treated as a dissonance. Vertical dissonances include normal and accented passing and neighbor tones, double-neighbor groups, and appoggiaturas.

2. Vertical sonorities are predominantly the octave and fifth, especially at the beginnings and endings of phrases. Triads also are common but not at phrase endings.

3. Oblique motion is most common, especially in pieces with a *cantus firmus*; contrary motion ranks second; parallel motion may involve any intervals, including fourths, fifths, and occasionally octaves or unisons. The harmonic interval of the tritone is usually avoided.

4. Cadences generally involve movement into the octave and fifth by step.

TONALITY

1. Melody and harmony are governed by the modal system, rather than the tonal system of major and minor.

2. Most pieces establish a strong feeling of tonic, governed by the mode of the part indicated as the *tenor*. It is often a preexisting chant or secular melody.

Structural Dimension

TEXTURE

1. Monophonic music consists of chant, solo song, and instrumental dances.

2. In music for two or more parts, polyphonic textures are more prevalent than homophonic textures.

3. The number of parts rarely exceeds four. Polyphonic music is usually in two or three parts.

4. Textures are often created by adding new parts to existing parts with frequent crossing of voices.

MAJOR GENRES

1. Choral music: sacred genres are the chant, organum, motet, conductus, hymn settings, and mass movements. Secular genres are songs of the troubadours and other court musicians, and the fixed song forms (the *ballade*, *rondeau*, and *virelai* in France and the *ballata*, the medieval madrigal, and the *caccia* in Italy).

2. Dance music: the *estampie*, *ductia*, and *saltarello*, for solo and ensemble.

STRUCTURAL DEVICES

1. As mentioned above, polyphonic motets and mass movements were often constructed by adding new parts to existing parts (*cantus firmi* or *tenor parts* from older works).

2. Repetition, variation, and sequence are commonly used devices.

3. Canon is used in the *caccia* and in works by Dufay and other fifteenth-century composers.

4. Fixed forms are used for the various types of secular songs.

Color Dimension

DYNAMICS AND ARTICULATION

1. Dynamics and articulation are to be inferred by performers and transcribers, since they are not indicated in the score.

2. Coloristic effects are achieved by combining sustained parts, such as a *cantus firmus*, with active parts, frequent part crossing, and use of *hocket*.

SCORING AND INSTRUMENTATION

1. Instrumental accompaniment for choral music is not indicated. Doubling of parts by organ or other instruments, however, probably occurred on occasions.

2. Specific instrumentation is not given for ensemble music. Music for keyboard and for plucked instruments does not name specific instruments in most cases.

3. Today, early music ensembles make very colorful use of reproductions of early instruments, doubling, addition of drones, and improvised ornamentation.

STYLE PROFILE: RENAISSANCE

Temporal Dimension

METER AND PULSE

1. The medieval system of *mensural notation* continues to govern meter. The time signature governs the relationship between levels of note values. The beats (*tactus*) are grouped or subdivided in threes ("perfect") or twos ("imperfect"). Measure bars are not used until the seventeenth century. If the beats are grouped in threes and subdivided in twos, the meter in a modern transcription would be $\frac{6}{8}$.

2. Meters most often found in early Renaissance music are $\frac{3}{4}$ or $\frac{6}{8}$ in modern transcription.

3. In mid- and late-Renaissance music, the most common meters are $\frac{4}{4}$, $\frac{4}{2}$, or ¢ in modern transcription, with faster sections written in $\frac{3}{2}$ meter.

4. In much of the sacred music, the feeling of what we call "measure accent" is not very strong, and the music flows without a strong pulse.

5. In secular vocal music the pulse may be more marked, and it is strong in Renaissance dance music.

6. Hemiola is occasionally encountered.

RHYTHM

1. Except for long notes at the ends of major sections, a relatively limited range of note values is used. A typical motet in transcription rarely uses note values larger than the whole note or smaller than the eighth note.

2. Phrases tend to begin with longer notes, then proceed to a variety of note values.

3. Rhythms tend to de-emphasize a regular accentuation of the down beat.

4. Rhythmic motion is equally distributed among the parts (except when a part is assigned to a cantus firmus).

Pitch Dimension

MELODY

1. Predominantly stepwise; leaps are rarely larger than an octave; leap of a major sixth is rare; leaps of a tritone, major or minor seventh, major or minor ninth, and all augmented or diminished intervals are discouraged.

2. Primarily diatonic; degree inflection is ruled by the principles of *musica ficta* (raising of the leading tone at cadences in Dorian and Aeolian modes, lowering B to B♭ to avoid the tritone).

3. After larger leaps (sixth, octave) the melody proceeds by step in the opposite direction.

4. Common dissonant figures: passing tone, neighbor tone, double-neighbor, cambiata, and suspension.

5. Long, often melismatic phrases are used in the masses, motets, and canticle settings; shorter, more syllabic phrases are used in chansons, madrigals, canzonas, and most instrumental music.

6. Repetition, sequence, and periodic structures are more common in secular than in sacred music

HARMONY

1. Consonance/Dissonance ratio is generally 3 or 4 to 1. Nonharmonic tones are limited to those listed in Item 4 above.

2. Vertical sonorities are predominantly major and minor triads. The diminished triad is used in first inversion.

3. Root motion by step, third, fourth, and fifth are found in nearly equal abundance.

4. Authentic, plagal, half, and deceptive cadences are all used as well as modal cadences (especially the Phrygian). By the end of the period, the authentic cadence becomes most common.

TONALITY

1. Melody and harmony are governed by the modal system, rather than the tonal system of major and minor. Tonal focus is achieved melodically at cadences.

2. The concept of a "tonic key" for a piece does not appear until the seventeenth century.

Structural Dimension

TEXTURE

1. Polyphonic textures are more prevalent than homophonic textures, which are often used to provide contrast.

2. All parts are of equal importance in most polyphonic genres.

MAJOR GENRES

1. Choral music: sacred genres are the mass, the motet, settings of the Passion, the Lamentations, hymns, antiphons, and the canticles (especially the Magnificat). Secular genres are the chanson and the madrigal.

2. Solo music: imitative pieces (ricercar, canzona, fantasia) and variation sets for keyboard and for lute are common, as well as songs for lute and voice.

3. Instrumental ensemble music consists mainly of the ricercar, canzona, fantasia, and various dances.

STRUCTURAL DEVICES

1. Use of the techniques of sequence, inversion, imitation, and canon are pervasive. Homophonic music ("familiar style") is used for contrast and in simple dance-like pieces.

2. Variation types are used frequently in instrumental music. Cantus firmus variations are common, as are dance variations. Variations often make use of the melodic elaboration technique referred to as "divisions."

3. Periodic structures (antecedent, consequent) are relatively uncommon, except for songs and dance music.

Color Dimension

DYNAMICS AND ARTICULATION

1. Dynamics and articulation are to be inferred by performers and transcribers, since they are not indicated in the score.

2. Sections in homophonic texture and music for larger number of parts are usually interpreted at higher dynamic levels.

SCORING AND INSTRUMENTATION

1. Instrumental accompaniment for choral music is not indicated. Doubling of parts by instruments, however, probably occurred on occasions.

2. Specific instrumentation is not usually given for ensemble music. Music for keyboard and for plucked instruments does not name specific instruments in most cases.

3. Shifts in the number of parts, melismatic to syllabic text setting, and polyphonic to homophonic textures are used for coloristic variety.

4. Music involving strong emotions such as sorrow, pain, and fear makes liberal use of the suspension.

STYLE PROFILE: BAROQUE

Temporal Dimension

METER AND PULSE

1. Baroque music uses the standard meters generally in the range of $\frac{3}{8}$ through $\frac{4}{4}$.

2. A strong, steady pulse with regular metric accents is maintained (except for the recitatives).

3. In opera, oratorio, and cantata recitatives, the beat is suspended to accommodate the vocal part.

RHYTHM

1. The range of note values in a piece or movement is relatively small. When eighth notes carry the motion, quarters or sixteenths also will be numerous. Larger and smaller note values will be fewer. Baroque music, however, may use any of the standard note values from whole notes to thirty-second notes.

2. Motivic figures often move toward the down beat.

3. Highly ornamented melodies make use of a large variety of rhythmic figures.

4. The continuo bass moves in steady eighths or quarters to accompany more rhythmically diverse upper parts.

5. Rhythmic motion is equally distributed among the parts in polyphonic genres such as the fugue, although one part may be distinguished from the others as a cantus firmus.

Pitch Dimension

MELODY

1. Mostly stepwise, but leaps of all kinds are used freely. Leaps of augmented or diminished intervals are usually chord members.

2. Primarily diatonic, but chromaticism involved in modulation is used freely.

3. Motivic development and sequence are common features.

4. Appoggiaturas, accented passing and neighbor tones, retardations, and escape tones are added to the dissonant figures inherited from the Renaissance (passing, neighbor, double-neighbor, and suspension). The cambiata figure is found infrequently by 1700.

5. Range rarely exceeds a twelfth (except for highly virtuosic music).

6. Melody often outlines the prevailing harmony, filling the intervals between basic and harmonically associated pitches with passing tones and neighbor tones.

HARMONY

1. Consonance/Dissonance ratio is generally 2 or 3 to 1. Nonharmonic tones include all those listed in Item 4 above.

2. Vertical sonorities include all types of triads and seventh chords. The dominant seventh chord is common by the middle of the period. The diminished seventh chord often has a dominant function.

3. Root motion by step, fourth, and fifth are most common. Root movement by third is much less common.

4. The authentic cadence is almost exclusively used at strong cadences. Half and deceptive cadences also are common. Plagal and modal cadences are rare.

5. Secondary dominant chords, the Neapolitan sixth chord, and the augmented sixth chords are used frequently.

6. Harmonic rhythm is very stable. Once established, it changes very little except for a quickening at cadences.

TONALITY

1. The tonal system of major and minor is now firmly in place.

2. The tonality remains strong, even when there are frequent modulations.

3. Modulation to closely related keys is commonplace; modulation to remote keys is quite rare, even in Bach's chromatic works.

Structural Dimension

TEXTURE

1. The period begins with a preference for homophonic textures. By the time of Bach, however, polyphonic textures have gained the edge.

2. The continuo is used almost universally. Exceptions are solo keyboard music, early madrigals by Monteverdi, a cappella motets by Schütz, and English consort music.

MAJOR GENRES

1. Choral music: sacred genres are the cantata, oratorio, mass, motet, anthem, Magnificat and Passion setting, and Service. Secular genres are the late madrigal and choruses from opera, secular oratorio, and cantata.

2. Solo instrumental genres are sonatas, suites, preludes, fugues, toccatas, passacaglias, and variation sets for keyboard, for solo instrument and continuo, and for solo instrument unaccompanied.

3. Solo vocal music is mainly found in opera, oratorio, and cantata arias. The *da capo aria* is the form most commonly used for solo arias.

4. Instrumental ensemble music: concerto grosso, concerto with solo instruments, orchestral suite, trio sonata.

STRUCTURAL DEVICES

1. Polyphonic music makes use of the fugal devices of imitation, inversion, canon, and to a lesser degree, augmentation and diminution.

2. Pervasive use of the sequence.

3. Much of the music makes use of the technique of *Fortspinnung,* "spinning out" of melodic material derived from a small set of motives.

4. Various techniques include ornamentation, change in harmonization, mode, or meter; variations may be based on a passcaglia bass or on a given harmonic progression.

Color Dimension

DYNAMICS AND ARTICULATION

1. Dynamic markings are given in the original scores rather infrequently. Dynamics tend to be "terraced"—at fixed levels, rather than gradually changing.

2. Some articulations are indicated, but staccato and accent markings are rare.

SCORING AND INSTRUMENTATION

1. Instruments are indicated in the original scores. Some works, however, may be performed by a choice of instruments (violin, oboe, or recorder, for example).

2. Virtuosic vocal and instrumental music becomes quite common with the development of opera and improvements in instrumental design and performance technique.

3. A large variety of types and sizes of instruments allows for colorful scoring.

STYLE PROFILE: CLASSICAL

Temporal Dimension

METER AND PULSE

1. All standard meters are used, but $\frac{2}{4}$, $\frac{3}{4}$, $\frac{4}{4}$, and $\frac{6}{8}$ are most common.

2. A strong, steady pulse is maintained, but it may be tempered by ritardando or accelerando markings, especially in Beethoven's music.

3. In opera recitatives, the beat is suspended to accommodate the vocal part.

RHYTHM

1. The range of note values may be small or large, depending on the tempo and dramatic content of the music.

2. Motivic figures often move away from the down beat, due to frequent use of appoggiaturas.

3. In keyboard works, melody with a high rhythmic profile is often accompanied by simple patterns, such as the Alberti Bass.

Pitch Dimension

MELODY

1. Mostly stepwise, but leaps of all kinds are used freely. Leaps of augmented or diminished intervals may be harmonic or the result of appoggiaturas.

2. Primarily diatonic, but decorative chromaticism is common.

3. Graceful ornamentation is a common feature.

4. The full complement of dissonant figures is evident with increased use of the appoggiatura.

5. Range rarely exceeds a twelfth but occasionally endulges in large register changes in solo vocal and instrumental music.

6. Melody often outlines the prevailing harmony with arpeggiation.

HARMONY

1. Consonance/Dissonance ratio is generally 2 or 3 to 1. Nonharmonic tones of all kinds are used, chiefly in the melody.

2. Vertical sonorities include all types of triads and seventh chords.

3. The primary triads are given priority.

4. Root motion by step, fourth, and fifth is most common. Third-related progressions appear more frequently toward the end of the period, especially in the music of Beethoven.

5. The authentic cadence is almost exclusively used at strong cadences with a strong preference for the V_{4-3}^{6-5} to I configuration. Half and deceptive cadences also are common. Plagal and modal cadences are rare. The appoggiatura cadence, where one or more appoggiaturas are used in upper parts against the tonic in the bass, is very common.

6. Secondary dominant chords, ninth chords, the Neapolitan sixth chord, and the augmented sixth chords are plentiful.

7. Harmonic rhythm is less stable than in the Baroque era and is often slower moving.

TONALITY

1. Key scheme is a decisive factor in the articulation of form.

2. Tonal centers are firmly established at the beginning of a work and before and after modulations.

3. Modulation to closely related keys is commonplace; modulation to remote keys is occasionally encountered, especially in Beethoven's works.

Structural Dimension

MAJOR GENRES

1. Choral music: sacred genres are works for soloists, chorus, and orchestra, including masses, settings of Marian antiphons, Latin hymns, and the Requiem, motets, and anthems. Secular genres include choruses from opera and part songs.

2. Solo (and solo with piano): sonatas, fantasias, and variation sets.

3. Solo vocal music: opera and concert arias, solo songs.

4. Instrumental ensemble music: symphonies, solo concertos, string quartets, trios (violin, cello, piano), and works for wind ensembles (serenades, divertimentos, cassations, and so on).

TEXTURE

1. Homophonic textures are more common than polyphonic textures.

2. Homophonic textures most often consist of melody with a high pitch and rhythmic profile in the uppermost part with simpler accompanying parts below.

3. When polyphonic textures are used, they resemble Baroque models and techniques.

STRUCTURAL DESIGN

1. Melodies (themes) are usually first presented in periodic structure.

2. The sonata-allegro form is normally used for the first movement of sonatas, trios, quartets, and symphonies. Sonata-allegro also may be used for the final movement and occasionally for the second movement.

3. Rondo forms are used most often for final movements.

4. Theme and variation may be used for any movement in larger works or for a single-movement work.

Color Dimension

DYNAMICS AND ARTICULATION

1. Dynamic markings are more consistently given than in scores from the Baroque era.

2. Crescendo and diminuendo markings are used more frequently than in the Baroque era.

3. Dramatic contrasts in dynamics are frequently encountered.

4. Articulation marks (phrasing, accents [*sfz*], staccato) appear more frequently.

SCORING AND INSTRUMENTATION

1. The art of orchestration develops strongly during the period, and composers make coloristic use of instrumentation.

2. With the further development of vocal technique and instrumental design and performance technique, composers could write highly virtuosic music.

STYLE PROFILE: ROMANTIC

Temporal Dimension

METER AND PULSE

1. All standard meters are used, but some experimentation with asymmetric meters can be seen.

2. A strong pulse is maintained, but markings such as *rubato, stretto, stringendo,* and *allargando* render the beat unsteady.

3. Dramatic tempo changes in a piece or movement are common.

RHYTHM

1. The range of note values varies, depending on the tempo and dramatic content of the music. Triplets are frequently used, as well as tuplets of five or more notes.

2. Rhythms of 2 against 3 are relatively common, especially in the music of Brahms.

3. The beat may be weakened by syncopations or off-beat accents.

Pitch Dimension

MELODY

1. Generally lyrical and expressive, often with longer phrases than earlier styles.

2. Often highly ornamented with scalar, chordal, or chromatic embellishments and virtuosic display.

3. The full complement of nonharmonic tones is evident with increased use of strong figures, such as appoggiaturas, which are often prolonged or approached by large leaps.

4. Colorful chord tones, such as the ninth or thirteenth and modal borrowings, are given melodic prominence.

HARMONY

1. Consonance/Dissonance ratio is generally about 2 to 1, but a higher proportion of dissonance may be found in the late nineteenth-century chromatic

works. Nonharmonic tones of all types are used, especially the accented and chromatic figures; nonharmonic tones may be found in any of the parts.

2. Increased use of chromatically altered harmonies such as the augmented triad, secondary dominant and diminished seventh chords, augmented sixth chords, Neapolitan sixth chords, extended dominants, and mutated chords.

3. Root motion by step, fourth, and fifth remains common, but third-related progressions appear frequently.

4. The authentic cadence continues to be used at strong cadence points, but deceptive or evaded cadences and irregular resolutions of dominant and diminished seventh chords are more plentiful.

5. Harmonic rhythm may be very stable or very unstable, depending on the mood of the music. Extended pedal points can slow down the harmonic rhythm dramatically. Modulating sequences and chromatic passages speed up the harmonic rhythm.

TONALITY

1. The key scheme for sonata-allegro and rondo forms may involve modulation to other keys than the dominant or relative major.

2. Tonal centers are not always firmly established at the beginning of a work.

3. Modulation to remote keys becomes more common.

4. Pervasive modulation in chromatic works tends to obscure the tonal focus.

5. Wagner's *Tristan Prelude* represents the beginning of a trend toward the eventual breakdown of tonality in the atonal works of Schoenberg and his followers.

Structural Dimension

MAJOR GENRES

1. Sacred choral music: works for soloists, chorus, and orchestra, masses, settings of the Requiem, and anthems. Secular genres: choruses from operas, oratorios, and part-songs.

2. Solo (and solo with piano): sonatas, variation sets, character pieces, etudes, preludes, and stylized sets of dances such as waltzes and mazurkas.

3. Solo vocal music: opera and concert arias, solo songs, and Lieder.

4. Instrumental ensemble music: symphonies, solo concertos, tone poems and other programmatic music, string quartets and quintets, piano quartets and quintets, trios (violin, cello, piano), and works for woodwind quartet and quintet.

TEXTURE

1. Homophonic textures are far more common than polyphonic textures. When polyphonic textures are used, they continue to resemble Baroque models but with Romantic harmony.

2. Melody with a figured harmonic accompaniment, very common in piano pieces, is applied to chamber ensembles and orchestra.

   3. A new polyphony arises wherein each part is allowed to move independently, changing the chord quality. The resulting series of chord mutations tends to obscure the tonality.

STRUCTURAL DESIGN

   1. Periodic structures remain common, but longer phrases and asymmetric periods also are frequently encountered.

   2. The sonata-allegro form is normally used for the first movement of multi-movement works. Sonata-allegro also may be used for the final movement and occasionally for the second movement.

   3. Themes become important to the articulation of form, in connection with key scheme.

   4. Theme and variation may be used for a larger work or for any movement of a symphony or concerto.

   5. Concertos no longer use the double exposition in the first movement. Cadenzas written by the composer become integral parts of the works.

Color Dimension

DYNAMICS AND ARTICULATION

   1. Composers show much more detail in dynamics, phrasing, articulation, and pedaling; "hair pins" are used to show detailed nuances of expression.

   2. The range of dynamics is expanded.

   3. Sudden dramatic contrasts in dynamics are frequently encountered.

SCORING AND INSTRUMENTATION

   1. Major works call for larger orchestral and choral forces.

   2. Developments in instrumental design: improved fingering for woodwinds, valves for brass instruments, a larger array of percussion instruments, improvements in range, dynamic capabilities, and mechanical action of the piano.

A GUIDE TO FIGURED BASS REALIZATION

A system was developed in the early Baroque era for the accompaniment of solo song, called the *basso continuo*. It consisted of the bass line with figures representing harmonies to be played on the accompanying instrument, serving the same purpose as today's lead sheet. The players improvised their accompaniment using the symbols as a guide. The continuo realization in Ex. B-1 is by a pupil of Bach and gives us a good idea of late Baroque practice.

Example B-1 Trio Sonata from *The Musical Offering* by J. S. Bach, continuo realization by J. P. Kirnberger.

Example B-1 (*continued*)

A. GENERAL GUIDELINES

1. Determine the harmonic rhythm. Decide where chord changes are likely to occur. If the bass consists of long notes, there may be one or more harmonies per note. If the bass moves in eighth notes or sixteenth notes or is arpeggiated, there may be several notes to a single chord.

2. Since the system is a kind of "shorthand" notation, not all details will be indicated. Some figured basses give only a few symbols to indicate unexpected harmonic events. Some continuo parts are unfigured and depend on the player's instinct and deduction from the musical context.

3. All symbols that appear indicate specific pitch classes to be played. Numbers indicate notes by interval above the bass, with or without intervening octaves. A 3 indicates a third, tenth, or seventeenth, for example.

4. Numbers indicate interval size; interval quality is affected by the signature. With a signature of one sharp, a 7 above G in the bass indicates F♯, a major 7th (14th, etc.) above. A 7 above D in the bass indicates a C, a minor 7th (14th, and so on) above.

5. A flat, sharp, or natural by itself or on the bottom of a column shows the alteration of the 3rd (10th, 17th, and so on) *above the bass*. It indicates the *chord third* only when the bass note is the root (see Ex. B-1, measures 6 and 8).

6. Any number that has a slash mark through it indicates that it is to be raised by a half step (see Ex. B-1, measure 7, and Ex. B-3, measure 1).

7. A flat, sharp, or natural that appears immediately next to a number (usually after it) indicates how the interval is to be altered (see Ex. B-1, measures 1 and 2).

8. When two or more numbers appear in succession for a single bass note, they indicate voice motion (see Ex. B-6). The symbols 4 3 below a C in the bass with no signature indicate melodic motion of F-E. The symbols 7 6 below a D with a signature of one flat indicate C-B♭.

9. Columns of figures are always given in descending numerical order from top to bottom (see Ex. B-5). This does not mean, however, that the chord members must be voiced in that order. In root position, the chord third, fifth, or a doubled root may be chosen as the highest note.

10. Figures appearing in continuo parts mean the same as those used with roman numeral chord analysis. A stack of figures that would not be found in roman numeral analysis generally indicates that the bass note is nonharmonic or that it is functioning as a pedal tone (see Ex. B-1, measure 7).

11. Horizontal lines indicate that the harmony is to be sustained while the bass moves.

B. IDENTIFYING TRIADS IN ROOT POSITION

Example B-2 A continuo part indicating only root position harmonies.

1. If a chord is expected and there are no figures, a diatonic root-position triad is indicated. This is the case for the two chords in the first measure of Ex. B-2.

2. A triad in root position may be indicated by a 3, a 5, or by $\frac{5}{3}$.

3. When a 4 appears above the bass note, it indicates a suspension or appoggiatura, and the next figure will indicate the resolution, a 3 or an accidental (showing the third is altered).

4. The figure 5 in a diminished triad is often indicated as an alteration (see Ex. B-1, measure 2, beat 3).

C. IDENTIFYING TRIADS IN INVERSION

Example B-3 Figures indicating first inversion.

1. A 6 indicates a triad in first inversion. The figure 6 implies a sixth and a third above the bass note. Occasionally both figures are given: $\frac{6}{3}$.

2. The figures 7 6 indicate a suspension or appoggiatura a seventh above the bass, resolving down a step to a sixth. This is often the uppermost voice.

3. Second inversion triads are indicated by the symbol $\frac{6}{4}$.

4. Altered chord members are shown by slashed numbers or added accidentals.

Example B-4 Second inversion triads in various configurations.

D. IDENTIFYING SEVENTH CHORDS

Example B-5 Seventh chords in various positions.

1. The figures 7, $^6_5$, $^4_3$, and $^4_2$ represent seventh chords in root position, first, second, and third inversion respectively. Third inversion is sometimes indicated by the figure 2 alone.

2. The full set of figures are occasionally used, and any altered chord members will be noted (see Ex. B-5).

E. IDENTIFYING NONHARMONIC TONES

Example B-6 Passage showing nonharmonic tones in the solo melody and how they are shown and realized in the continuo.

1. When the solo or ensemble being accompanied has a strong dissonance such as a suspension or appoggiatura, the figured bass symbols must show it, since ignoring it would result in unnecessary clashes. Number sequences such as 9 8, 7 6, 6 5, and 4 3 are the most common. The continuo player has the option of doubling the dissonant note or allowing the other instruments to play it. It is important, however, that the note of resolution is not played at the same time as the suspension or appoggiatura.

2. Occasionally there are two tones suspended or acting as appoggiaturas. Figures such as $\begin{smallmatrix} 6 & 5 \\ 4 & 3 \end{smallmatrix}$ and $\begin{smallmatrix} 9 & 8 \\ 4 & 3 \end{smallmatrix}$ are examples (see Ex. B-4 and B-6).

3. When the bass note itself is not a member of the harmony (accented passing tone, appoggiatura, and so on), a set of figures results that is not easily recognized, as are the figures for triads and seventh chords. Since the next note in the bass will most likely be a chord tone that is a step lower, raising each number by one will reveal the resulting harmony when the bass has moved. For example, $\begin{smallmatrix} 5 \\ 2 \end{smallmatrix}$ will become $\begin{smallmatrix} 6 \\ 3 \end{smallmatrix}$ when the bass moves down by step.

4. When the bass serves as a pedal tone, harmonies moving above it will result in unusual sets of figures (see Ex. 5-1, measure 7).

F.   SUGGESTIONS FOR VOICING IN A KEYBOARD CONTINUO REALIZATION

1. Avoid duplicating the solo or other instrumental parts in the right hand.

2. A four-part texture (including the bass) is appropriate for larger ensembles and for forte passages. A three-part texture is suitable for solo with continuo and for softer sections.

3. Let the left hand be assigned to the bass, and let the right hand have the harmony. Best results are obtained by moving the hands in contrary motion as much as possible.

4. Double the root more than any other chord member. Do not double altered tones.

5. It is best not to double the bass note when the symbol below it is 6, $\begin{smallmatrix} 6 \\ 5 \end{smallmatrix}$, or $\begin{smallmatrix} 4 \\ 2 \end{smallmatrix}$.

6. Avoid parallel octaves or fifths between the bass and the realization. Occasional parallel unisons or octaves between the realization and the solo part may be used.

7. Follow the principles of good voice leading and doubling in the right-hand part.

8. A smooth, legato effect can be achieved by tying common tones between chords.

9. When a chord is to be repeated, it may be desirable to rearrange its voicing for the sake of variety.

10. Decorative pitches may be added as long as they do not call too much attention to the continuo part.

11. "Make room" for the solo part by assigning the right-hand part to a somewhat different tessitura.

12. Keep the notes of the realization within a comfortable range for the hand. Chords should not exceed the span of an octave for the right hand.

GLOSSARY

Active tones. Scale degrees that call for melodic motion (TI-do, FA-mi, LA-so, and so on)

Alap. The opening section of a North Indian raga, performed without regular pulse or meter, that defines the character of the raga.

Amplitude. The sound pressure at the crest of a sound wave perceived by the listener as loudness or loudness.

Anacrucis. One or more notes preceding the first full measure of a piece or phrase, also called *pick-up* or *upbeat.*

Anticipation. A nonharmonic tone that is sounded before it becomes a part of the harmony when repeated.

Appoggiatura. A dissonant tone, usually sounded on a strong beat, which is approached by leap and resolved downward by step.

Applied dominants. See *secondary dominants.*

Asymmetric meters. Meters whose beats are of different lengths. Example: $\frac{7}{8}$ with beats of 3, 2, and 2 eighths' duration.

Atonality. The absence of tonality or tonal center. Atonal music is also described as nontonal.

Augmentation. Lengthening a melodic unit, especially a fugue subject, by multiplying its note values by a factor of two or more.

Auxiliary tone. See *neighbor tone.*

Basic pitches. Tones of structural importance in a melody.

Basso continuo. The bass line and chordal accompaniment in Baroque music, usually provided by a keyboard instrument and a bass instrument. See also *figured bass.*

Beat (metrical). The feeling of pulse to which we "keep time" to a piece of music; the metrical unit shown by conducting gestures.

Beats (acoustical). A pulsating sensation caused by two tones of nearly the same frequency as they go in and out of phase.

Binary. Twofold. Binary structures have two parts. The scheme may be A–B, where the second section is in contrast to the first, or A–A', where the second section is a variant of the first. Each section may be repeated.

Bitonal. Simultaneous use of two tonalities or keys.

Blue notes. Notes traditionally lowered in blues style melody, usually the third and seventh degrees of the major scale.

Borrowed chords. Chords are "borrowed" from a parallel mode to replace diatonic chords. Examples: a major subdominant used in the minor mode; a minor dominant used in the major mode.

Cambiata. *Nota cambiata* or changing note, a three- or four-note figure used mainly in fifteenth- and early sixteenth-century polyphony consisting of a step down, leap of a third down, step up. The second note of the group is dissonant with other parts.

Canon. Strict imitation of one part by one or more other parts sustained throughout a work or a section of a work. Imitation may be at the unison, octave, or other interval (most often perfect fourth or fifth), and the distance in time between leader and follower(s) remains fixed (a beat, a half measure, a measure, multiple measures, and so on).

Cantus firmus. A preexisting melody, often presented in long note values, to which counterpoint may be added. Chants and chorales are the most common.

Cents. Measurement of intervals smaller than a semitone or half step. There are 100 cents in 1 semitone.

Changing note. See *cambiata.*

Chord planing. Movement of all chord members in parallel sustained throughout a phrase or other melodic unit.

Church modes. Scale structures other than major and minor used during the Middle Ages and Renaissance, in much of Western folk music, and in the twentieth century. Also called *ecclesiastical modes,* their names have been borrowed from the Greek modal system: Dorian, Phrygian, Lydian, Mixolydian, and Aeolian.

Conjunct and disjunct motion. Melodic motion by step and by leap.

Complementary tones. See *nonharmonic tones.*

Cross-relation. The dissonance caused by the close proximity in two different voices of a diatonic pitch and an altered form of that pitch. Example: E♮ and E♭.

Da capo aria. The most common form of aria in dramatic vocal and choral works of the seventeenth and eighteenth centuries with the scheme A–B–A'. The final section features an ornamented version of the melody of the first section.

Decorative pitches. Pitches other than the basic structural pitches that give character to the texture. They may be harmonically related or nonharmonic.

Degree inflection. Free alteration by half step of any scale degrees with the exception of the tonic.

Double neighbor. A four-note melodic figure in which the second note is the upper neighbor and the third note is the lower neighbor to the first and fourth. The lower neighbor may come before the upper neighbor as well.

Échappée. See *escape tone.*

Envelope. Change over time of the amplitude, frequency, or timbre of a tone. Envelope is usually described in terms of attack time, steady state, and decay time.

Escape tone. A nonharmonic tone that is the second note in a three-note melodic figure consisting of a step up and a third down. Example: D–E–C, where E is nonharmonic. Also called *échappée*.

Extended chords. Dominant seventh chords with added ninth, eleventh, or thirteenths.

FIgured bass. A system of numbers and other symbols given with a bass line to specify harmonies to accompany the notated parts. See Appendix B.

Frequency. The number of cycles per second of a wave, perceived by the listener as pitch.

Fundamental. The lowest tone or the *first partial* in a harmonic series.

Gahu. A type of African percussion ensemble music.

Gaida. Bagpipe ornamentation in Balkan folk music.

Gamelan. Javanese and Balinese ensemble music.

Ground bass. A succession of tones in the bass over which variations are created.

Harmonic rhythm. The rate of harmonic change, usually expressed in the number of harmonic changes per measure.

Harmonic series. The fundamental (frequency f) and all overtones (2f, 3f, 4f, 5f, 6f, and so on) present in a complex tone. All members of the harmonic series are called *partials*.

Hemiola. 3:2 ratio. A musical gesture wherein a rhythmic figure with a duple metric pules replaces one with a triple metric pulse.

Heterophony. The simultaneous performance of two or more different versions of a single melody.

Hirajoshi. A five-note pitch collection represented by the syllables DO, RE, ME, SO, LE. It also is called the *minor pentatonic scale.*

Homophony. Melody with subordinate accompanying parts.

Indeterminacy. Some aspects of the music are left to chance or to free choice by the performers.

Interference (acoustical). The nulling effect caused by two waves that are 180° out of phase. The effect is most noticeable when the waves have the same frequency and amplitude.

Interval class. An interval and its inversion identified by the number of semitones it contains. Example: Interval class 4 = M3 and m6 (the M3 encompasses four semitones).

Inversion. Turned upside down, rendering each melodic interval in the opposite direction.

Lead sheet. A term used in jazz and popular music for the notation of a melody with chord symbols.

Meter. The organization of the beat or tactus into regularly recurring patterns of stresses and unstresses, also called the *time signature.*

Microtonal music. Music featuring intervals built on fractions of semitones.

MIDI. Musical Instrument Digital Interface. A digital protocol that specifies pitch, velocity, and other tonal aspects recognized by synthesizers, computer music programs, and other digital musical devices.

Minimalist music. Music based on limited and gradually changing repetitions of rhythmic, harmonic, and melodic patterns.

Mode. (1) In general, any diatonic scale, including major and minor (2) One of the church modes (Dorian, Phrygian, Lydian, Mixolydian, Aeolian).

Modulation. The process of changing from one key to another.

Monophony. Unaccompanied melody.

Motive. The smallest unit of music that has enough character to be subsequently developed.

Multiphonics. Two or more pitches sounded simultaneously on a single wind instrument.

Musique concrète. Recorded sounds that are processed by various means including tape speed changes, tape reversal, tape editing, electronic filtering, ring modulation, mixing, and assembled into a composition.

Neighbor tone. A tone that is a step above or below the pitch that precedes and follows it. It is called *auxiliary tone* as well.

Nonharmonic tones. Decorative pitches that are not members of the harmony that accompanies them. Also called *complementary tones.*

Octatonic scale. A scale that alternates whole and half steps. Also called the *diminished scale.* The step sequence may begin with either a whole or half step.

Ostinato. A repeating figure, often in the bass, but possible in any part. See *ground bass* and *passacaglia.*

Overtones. Harmonics or partials above the fundamental pitch of a complex tone. The relative strength of the overtones contributes to the perception of tone quality.

Pandiatonicism. Free use of the tones of a diatonic scale without regard to traditional functional harmony.

Partials. Members of the harmonic series.

Passacaglia. A set of continuous variations on a repeating bass line. See *ground bass* and *ostinato.*

Passing tone. A nonharmonic pitch that connects by step two harmonic pitches a third apart. Example: C–D–E, where C and E are harmonic and D is the passing tone. Two passing tones may occur next to each other. Example: E–F♯–G♯–A or C–B♮–B♭–A.

Pentatonic collection. A five-note pitch collection represented by the syllables DO, RE, MI, SO, LA.

Pelog. One of two tuning systems, the other being *slendro,* used in a Javanese gamelan The system contains seven pitches. Three-to five-note figures are also called *pelog.* See also *slendro.*

Period. Two or more phrases that form a cohesive unit, with the last phrase ending in a more conclusive cadence than any that precede it.

Phrase. A relatively complete musical idea ending with some kind of cadence.

Picardy Third. Alteration of the third of a tonic minor chord changing its quality to major. It is often found as the final chord in a piece or section in the minor mode.

Pitch class. All pitches with the same letter name or numeric name, regardless of register. All Cs on a piano are *pitch class* C. All Cs can be identified as *pitch class* 0 (zero).

Pointillism. A term borrowed from painting technique to describe a musical texture in which notes are isolated from one another by rhythmic spaces and register.

Polychord. A vertical sonority consisting of the combination of two or more simple chords, usually triads. Example: C, E, G, A, C♯, E.

Polyphony. Music for two or more voices or parts in a contrapuntal texture.

Polytonality. Simultaneous use of two or more tonal centers. Each tonal center is associated with a key, mode, or independent pitch collection. See *bitonal.*

Portamento. A continuous glide in pitch from one note to the next.

Quartal harmony. In the strict sense, harmony based on the interval of the perfect fourth, rather than the third, as in tertian harmony; in a broader sense, music in which the perfect fourth, major second, and minor seventh are treated like consonances (as well as the perfect unison, octave, and fifth, and the major and minor thirds and sixths).

Rag(a). Mode, melodic patterns, and mood in music of India.

Regional progression. A succession of harmonies that temporarily establishes a key that is closely related to the original key.

Resonance. The amplification of sound gained when a vibrating body is connected to an enclosed space or system that fits the wave length of the vibrations; the increase in volume gained by transmitting vibrations to a solid medium such as a sound board.

Retardation. A tone that becomes dissonant when suspended over a change of harmony, then resolves upward to make a consonance. The most common retardation figure involves the suspension of TI that resolves to DO.

Secondary dominant chords. Chords with a dominant relationship to diatonic triads other than the tonic. Also called *applied dominant chords.*

Senza mesura. Literally, "music without measures." Music in which there is little or no feeling of metrical organization.

Serial music. Music in which a series of pitches governs the construction of melody and harmony instead of the tonal system. In twelve-tone serial music, a tone row consisting of all twelve pitch classes of the chromatic scale is used as the basis of composition. Serial technique is sometimes extended to rhythm, dynamics, or other musical parameters.

Sequence. The repetition of a musical idea at one or more different pitch levels.

Simultaneity. (1) Two or more pitches sounded together. (2) A texture created by the sounding together of two or more unrelated musical ideas.

Sine wave. The simple wave form having no overtones.

Slendro. One of two tuning systems, the other being *pelog,* used in a Javanese gamelan. The system contains five pitches. See also *pelog.*

Solfège. A system used as an aid in identifying and expressing the aural quality of the various scale degrees. Also called the *sol-fa system.*

Stable tones. Tones on scale degrees 1, 3, and 5 that are normally the goal of melodic motion.

Suspension. A tone that becomes dissonant when suspended over a change of harmony, then resolves downward to make a consonance.

Syncopation. A rhythmic figure in which notes are sounded on weak beats and sustained through strong beats.

Tactus. The beat level at which we "keep time" to the music. This is the beat level that is best for conducting.

Tal. The second part of a North Indian raga where a regular metrical pulse begins. At this point the tabla joins the ensemble.

Temperament (acoustic). Tuning system. In equal temperament, all half steps have the same frequency ratio.

Ternary. Threefold. Ternary structures have three parts. The scheme is A–B–A, where the final section may be a varied repetition of the first.

Tertian harmony. Harmony based on thirds, or triadic harmony, the basis of the tonal system of the common practice period.

Third relation. Chords whose roots are a third apart. Third-related chords using only diatonic triads have two common tones. When there is but one common tone, chromatic alteration will be required. When there are no common tones, the harmonic effect is very striking, and the tonality may become ambiguous.

Tonality. Music in which the pitches exhibit a relationship to a tonal center or tonic. The tonic exerts an attraction on the other pitches not unlike the sun for the planets in the solar system.

Tuplet. Any grouping of notes that goes against the expected division or subdivision of the meter or the beat. Most common is the triplet that has three notes in the space of two.

Wave length. The distance between the crest of one cycle of a periodic wave and the next.

Index

Page numbers in italics refer to musical examples.